Best wishes from Macey Hill

Very best wishes William Hague

Bath 27/7/00.

Contemporary Writing and National Identity

Contemporary
Writing and
National Identity

Edited by
Tracey Hill
and
William Hughes

First published in 1995 by

SULIS PRESS
Newton Park
Bath BA2 9BN

Printed by
Antony Rowe Ltd.,
Chippenham

British Library Cataloguing in Publication Data

A catalogue record for this book is available
from the British Library

ISBN: 0 9526856 0 4

Contents

CONTENTS

Acknowledgements

The editors would like to thank the contributors for their patience and support throughout the publication of this volume. We are also grateful to colleagues at Bath College of Higher Education for their support and encouragement. Special thanks are due to Jon Press, whose help and advice were invaluable, to Neil Sammells for supporting the project so forcefully, to Paul Edwards for his professional copy-editor's eye, to Jeff Rodman for his comments and suggestions and to Richard Kerridge, for his comments on the Introduction, and for the cartoon on the front cover.

1

Introduction

Tracey Hill and William Hughes

> We cannot understand nations and nationalism simply as an ideology or
> form of politics, but must treat them as cultural phenomena as well. That
> is to say, nationalism, the ideology and movement, must be closely
> related to *national identity*, a multi-dimensional concept.[1]

In recent years, fundamental challenges and changes to national identity have
occurred: in Europe as a result of the break-up of the Soviet Union and other
Eastern European countries, in South Africa, and, even as we write, in Ireland,
Israel and Canada. Concurrently, writers and scholars have explored in ever
greater depth the forces and effects of nationalism, ethnicity and race.[2] This
volume of essays is a wide-ranging and valuable contribution to that exploration.
The chapters of this volume address the question of national identity from a
variety of disciplines and with a diversity of critical and methodological
perspectives.

The fragmentation of large polities by the move towards regionalism, and the
redrawing of national boundaries along ethnic rather than territorial lines are
political realities of our time. Contemporary writing cannot help but reflect and
problematise these changes; as Simon During has argued, literature can 'function
as a signifier of national identity or heritage'.[3] It is becoming increasingly
apparent that existing certainties about national identity no longer have the force
of old, and that they are being supplanted by a more flexible notion of national
belonging, based on quite different paradigms. This, it might be argued, is a
symptom of a postmodern condition, since postmodernity is nothing if it is not
a revisionist attitude towards a range of identities, individual *and* collective. It
would follow then, that, given this postmodern perspective, any attempt to arrest
such movement or to reinforce national identities currently under threat could be
regarded as a rejection of the notion of shifting or plural identity, and as a
pursuit of an ideal of closure. Furthermore, it seems likely that contemporary
writing that draws upon national identity would often be characterised by a sense
of loss and uncertainty. For instance, those who strive to retain the integrity of
the Union of Great Britain – itself a product of an historical process – and who

call for resistance to devolution, can be seen as the defenders of an ahistorical fiction of national unity.

National identity certainly has its fictional dimensions. A nation's history *is* a fiction, a construction by means of which a nation appropriates its past in order to assert the coherence and stability of its nationhood. As Homi Bhabha has so magisterially shown, nation depends implicitly upon narration: the idea of a nation has, like a text, 'textual strategies, metaphoric displacements, sub-texts and figurative stratagems'.[4] Clearly, national identity is never simply a matter of political or social affiliation. Recent instances of the revival or reinvention of nation states (the Baltic republics, for example) demonstrate how an awareness of the past can function as a model for the future. A sense of history has its part to play too in the way in which historically-specific versions of identity are invoked at times of crisis, such as the end of an empire. Present generations, Marx wrote, 'conjure up the spirits of the past and borrow from them names, battle-cries and costumes in order to present the new scene of world history in this time-honoured disguise and this borrowed language.'[5] Recurrent nationalisms can re-emerge, paradoxically, under the guise of postmodern fragmentation.

This can be seen as further evidence of the pressures of postmodernity. Since the Renaissance, the modern nation state has been the unit of political identification, secured through a combination of civil negotiation and military force, where the individual's relationship to that nation is based upon a model of citizenship. In contrast, an alternative form of identity might be founded rather on a sense of *ethnic* communality, based upon cultural traditions that conflict with hegemonic already-existing national identities. Asserting such a nationality implies the claim that a certain ethnic group has a 'right' to a specific geographical area, regardless of conventional and established territorial boundaries. What both manifestations of nationalism share, however, is what is common to nationalisms the world over: a fundamental exclusiveness, the form of which is binary. Claiming a particular national identity entails excluding all others: one is English because one is categorically *not* French, German or American, for example. Naturally, this presents severe ontological problems for those with what Dominic Williams calls 'hyphenated identities', such as Chinese-American, which infringe binarism. Similarly, one territory cannot belong to more than one nation at the same time – hence the tensions of ethnic conflict *within* a pre-existing state. It is, of course, characteristic of binaries that their stability is precarious. Great Britain is a case in point: one has to be both Scottish *and* British, Welsh and British, (perhaps most problematically) Irish and British, and, of course, English and British, although none of these combinations are possible without some discomfort.

2

The chapters of this volume all share this problematic modern context. Uniting the disparate accounts contained here is a common preoccupation with the *redefinition* of national identity, where national identity is perceived as no longer convincingly fixed or static, but rather fluid and polysemous. Reflecting the currently unstable circumstances of so many nation states and their associated ideologies, a range of texts and contexts is reappraised as these undergo change. The anatomies of past transformations are also examined comparatively, as they reveal a part of a continuing process of reworking and rewriting the constraints of national identity.

Given this context of disruption and flux, it is hardly surprising that the ways in which scholarship has approached questions of writing and national identity are complex and require some scrutiny. In this volume, three discrete cultural concepts – 'national', 'identity' and 'writing' – provide the focal points, although the relationship between these can fluctuate. These concepts in themselves are also highly variable, in that their definitions and contents may alter depending on the political or cultural context within which they can be shown to operate.

As has been suggested above, what constitutes 'national' at any given moment is not unproblematic. In *National Identity*, Anthony Smith identifies distinctive Western and Eastern versions of national identity: these are defined as 'culture communities' and 'a community of birth and native culture', respectively. The two are not, however, necessarily mutually exclusive, particularly in the traditional West. Language is an essential aspect of the communication and verification of both of these trends. The presence of rival languages within Western national communities may be seen to redirect their overall conception of the national into something that rather more resembles the Eastern or 'ethnic' idea of the nation. So, for instance, the experience of nominally bilingual communities, such of those of Wales or Ireland within Great Britain, might demand the revision of these arbitrary definitions. At this point, the question of what a postmodern national identity might look like is once more thrown into relief, since neither one predicated on ethnicity, nor on political affiliation, can withstand too much fragmentation. This instability is further compounded by other complex forms of national identity. Smith's notion of the Eastern model as a non-negotiable racial 'community of common descent' from which escape is impossible is disrupted by the experiences of both the colonised East and those who migrate in either direction.[6]

Identity, specifically communal identity, is made problematic not merely by an individual migrating from country to country, or from one self-consciously national group to another, but also by the existence of ambivalent groups who sit uneasily, if at all, within existing categories (an instance of this might be the Falashas, the black Ethiopian Jews who migrated to Israel during the mid-80s famine). There are also other components of identity which cross its increasingly permeable boundaries. National identity may, then, be conditioned or disrupted by factors outside the realms of the purely ethnic or geographical: for example, by sexuality or sexual identity, or by gender.[7] Gender politics present an inherent challenge to a fixed national identity, given the internationalist impulses of much contemporary feminism, the identification (by Woolf, for example) of nationalism, war and the like with masculinity, and other tensions, such as the complex situation of some women within Islamic populations. Such tangential concerns suggest the possibility not only of communities within communities, but of communities that transcend nationality – or proclaim themselves beyond its limitations. Another model for this type of problematic belonging might be the cultural stereotype (demonised so effectively in this century by fascist nationalisms) of the itinerant cosmopolitan artist or writer, who claims an affiliation above and beyond the national, and implicitly rejects the role of speaking on behalf of a people or race. Earlier examples of this might be Baudelaire, the metropolitan *flâneur*, Joyce and his modernist hostility towards nationality, or Walter Benjamin as the internationalist intellectual. More recently, post-modernism has provided an updated version: the Lyotardian *bricoleur*, one who 'listens to reggae, watches a western, eats McDonald's food for lunch and local cuisine for dinner, wears Paris perfume in Tokyo and "retro" clothes in Hong Kong',[8] all apparently without any concomitant national identification. Here, of course, the national and/or international dimension derives from the globalisation of late capitalism, rather than the socialist internationalism of the past.[9] A writer postioned outside the nation in this way has most often been constituted as a figure of irresponsibility or betrayal (*à la* Salman Rushdie) – but it can (as some of the chapters of this book demonstrate) indicate a witness of contemporary history who has a perilously frank gaze.

Writing too shows itself to be heterogeneous. What actually constitutes 'writing' – or the areas of writing generally encompassed by that term? Traditional literary criticism has expanded its remit to include the different cultural forms which are implicated in the construction of national identity. This movement away from the strictly 'literary' towards an accommodation of the kinds of texts conventionally excluded as sub- or extra-cultural (reportage, political tracts, letters and memoranda, amongst others) has expanded the limits of what 'writing' can refer to. These limits can be extended further still through explorations of the relationship between the word and image in other cultural forms (maps, wall-paintings, graffiti, Hollywood films) which can be regarded as having a role to play in expressions of perceived national differences. The relationship between writing and history is dynamic and cannot simply be reduced to text and background; as Neil Sammells has pointed out: 'writing creates, deploys and destroys the myths and images by which a people both sustain and imprison themselves.'[10] Hence the multiplicity of cultural texts and phenomena towards which our contributors turn.

National identity is thus shown to be irreducible to one single unified meaning. It is, as these chapters will demonstrate, subject to an unceasing process of redefinition and revision, a process in which this volume is playing a part. In their differently-inflected ways, the chapters that follow are all addressing this problematic.

*

In this century, the demise and reconstitution of the colonies of Western nations has seen an associated upheaval in the perceptions of nationhood emanating from both former colony and former coloniser. A number of these papers contain re-evaluations of colonial and post-colonial identities. Michael Parker's exploration of Derek Walcott's contribution to post-colonial writing charts the multiple tensions between Africa and the Caribbean. His essay shows how a reworking of the European languages of the former colonists has become a tool with which to define the cultural ambivalences of a location physically and politically between the Americas and Africa, and how Walcott's stance is made yet more complex by his attitudes towards women. Similarly, Dominic Williams, in his essay on Maxine Hong Kingston, considers the complexity of Chinese-American identity, and traces Kingston's resistance to being categorised as either, a position informed largely by her gender. David Ellis addresses the problematic situation of an Indo-Caribbean writer, David Dabydeen, relocated to the coloniser's country, Britain, again focusing on the question of language and one's place within it as a code of identity. From a post-structuralist perspective, Gail Low interrogates the alienation of V. S. Naipaul, a writer from a national similar context as Dabydeen, and shows how such alienation is manifested through the symbolic functions of the body in the works of Bharati Mukherjee. Gerry Smyth, in his exploration of contemporary Ireland, views its current situation as one midway between the colonial and post-colonial moment, and examines the role literary criticism has to play in this struggle.

Migrancy and emigration are central concerns of both Tracy Brain's and Colin Edwards's essays. Tracy Brain discusses how Sylvia Plath deals with her transatlantic location, bridging America and England, and how Plath negotiates an intrinsically unstable national identity. Problems of geographical movement are also interrogated in Colin Edwards's essay, where Ford Madox Ford's complicated Anglo-German identity at a time of international crisis is reviewed. In Peter Vujakovic's chapter, it is an entire country on the move that invites analysis: his case study is the former Yugoslavia, as it disintegrates and is reconfigured along ethnic lines, and the attempt of the Atlas of Croatia to arrest this disintegration.

To substantiate the idea raised above that national identity can be either consolidated or undermined by tangential factors such as gender, Clare Hanson's essay foregrounds the complex results of such encounters; she shows how Virginia Woolf couples gender with pacifism to expose another case of national belonging pushed to its limits. Gender is not the only disruptive element in the construction of identities: Richard Kerridge demonstrates this in his reading of contemporary novels and films, which delineates the irruption of social class into representations of Englishness, Germanness and Americanness. The latter two identities are further explored in Nicola King's essay, bringing together American fantasies of the Holocaust (fictive and memorial) and the place of Germany in contemporary European identity. While Richard Kerridge identifies postmodernity with late-capitalist America, Tim Middleton seeks to reveal the implications of the demise of modernity in recent Scottish writing, where subjectivity can be shown to be decentred and fragmented in the same way as national identity.

The remaining chapters are concerned with various aspects of Britain and its component parts. Through an examination of early-modern versus contemporary versions of the British Union, Willy Maley emphasises the contingency of this political formation in both pre- and post-union modes, and suggests the material consequences and implications of its existence for those included within it. In Tom Herron's essay on the importance of the powerful trope of 'the field' to contemporary Irish culture, the importance of non-literary media such as murals to a sense of nationality is again emphasised. Keeping to a British context, Simon Barker explores the versions of national identity propounded in a recent television serialisation of Michael Dobbs's novels of government, and as they are voiced by a major icon of that identity itself, the Queen. Barker goes on to question the place of stable nationhood as a prime form of identity in the face of the challenge of postmodernity and its theorists. Finally, Antony Easthope's essay further examines the function of the monarchy in the popular consciousness of British society and in the process revisits some of the theoretical perspectives raised in this Introduction. He appraises Englishness as a variant of Britishness, critiques the binary oppositions upon which these identities rest, and concludes with a polemical survey of contemporary political versions of national identity.

NOTES

1. Anthony D. Smith, *National Identity*, London 1991, vii.

2. See, for example, Edward Said, *Culture and Imperialism*, London 1993; Homi Bhabha, ed., *Nation and Narration*, London 1990; Linda Colley, *Britons*, New Haven 1992; Paul Hyland and Neil Sammells, eds., *Irish Writing: Exile and subversion*, Basingstoke 1991; Bill Ashcroft, Gareth Griffiths and Helen Tiffin, eds., *The Post-Colonial Studies Reader*, London 1995.

3. Simon During, 'Literature – nationalism's other? The case for revision', in Bhabha, ed., op. cit., 138.

4. ibid., 2. (See also Homi Bhabha, *The Location of Culture*, London 1994, *passim*.)

5. Karl Marx, 'The Eighteenth Brumaire of Louis Bonaparte', in David McLennan, ed., *Karl Marx: Selected writings*, Oxford 1977, 300.

6. Smith, op. cit., 11.

7. For an anecdotal account of the brittle relationships between sexual identity and a political-religious community, see C. Gebler, *The Glass Curtain: Inside an Ulster community*, London 1992, 11.

8. Jean-François Lyotard, trans. G. Bennington and B. Massumi, *The Postmodern Condition: A report on knowledge*, Manchester 1984, 76.

9. For further discussion of the way in which Marxism has dealt with the conflict between nationalism and internationalism, see Fredric Jameson, *The Political Unconscious: Narrative as a socially symbolic act*, London 1981, 298.

10. Neil Sammells, 'Introduction', *Irish Writing: Exile and subversion*, xiii.

2

Writing about writing and national identity

Gerry Smyth

Contemporary Writing and National Identity, Nation and Narration, Culture and Imperialism, Irish Writing and the Post-Colonial Moment – the 'and' which links the first and second elements of these and a plethora of other formulations concerning Irish cultural history has a history of its own, a history characterised by the struggle between various ways of comprehending the relationship between cultural texts and the specific geographical locations from which such texts emerge.[1] The main location of this historical struggle has been another form of writing – literary criticism. In other words, the concept of 'writing and national identity' and its myriad surrogates can only have significance when framed by a metadiscourse which purports to comment on, but actually constructs, the 'original' or 'primary' discourse. In this essay I wish to comment on the significance of the relationship between 'primary' and 'secondary' forms of writing in the context of modern Irish decolonisation, and assess what might be the implications of a deconstruction of received literary and critical practices for the 'Irish cultural tradition'.

It is generally accepted that culture, in the broadest possible sense, plays a vital role in the colonising and decolonising processes, and that certain kinds of subject, of which the writer and the critic are prominent examples, played a key role in the emergence of an Irish national identity in the nineteenth and twentieth centuries. Culture represents (in both senses) the most salient discourse wherein the battle for power in societies occurs; it frames, justifies, and gives form to the hegemonic struggles in which the subject acts. Cultural discourse, to adapt Foucault, is the power which is to be seized, and the seizure and redeployment of language and literature have historically constituted an indispensable tactic in any decolonising narrative.[2] But what is meant by 'culture' in this context, and what kind of role did it play in Irish decolonisation? The Irish penchant for *literary* activity has become a truism of twentieth-century intellectual debate. In fact, the story of the country's wonderful cultural heritage and its connection – paradoxically assured and uncertain – with its nationalist struggles is perhaps one of the dominant images through which Ireland has come to be known to the modern world. Swift is more famous than Grattan, as Yeats is more famous than

8

de Valera, as Seamus Heaney or Roddy Doyle are probably more famous than any current Irish politician. Especially after the cultural revival of the 1890s, literature and politics were assumed to be intimately associated practices, and this relationship came to constitute one of the nation's dominant self-formative images, supporting and supported by various forms of religious, economic, and political discourse. And yet, this seemingly natural relationship has a history; it emerged and continues to exist only as the result of struggles between different ways of figuring the relationship between an imagined national community and the cultural forms through which that community can know itself.

To repeat, the location of those struggles was literary criticism. Before the primary acts of nation could be performed, culture – and specifically that highly specialised organisation of codes and practices known as 'literature' – needed to be framed by a secondary, or *meta*, discourse which would allow it to participate in decolonising activity. In other words, there could be no national literature of resistance until a pre-figuring critical discourse created a series of social and institutional spaces in which such a literature and its particular effects could function and have meaning; and even after this literature is 'founded' and the Irish writer of the nineteenth and twentieth centuries became self-conscious of his/her role as the 'narrator' of the nation, literary criticism still played a crucial role in validating, refining and performing these narratives, and in facilitating or resisting the often violent transition between the different modes of decolonisation. As Edward Said writes: 'critics create not only the values by which art is judged and understood, but they embody in writing those processes and actual conditions in the *present* by means of which art and writing bear significance.'[3]

What I am suggesting, in the first instance, is that the historical and psychological relationships that have obtained between England and Ireland in the discourse of colonialism were replicated in the cultural field in the relationship between a 'primary' (art/culture/literature) and a 'secondary' (commentary/criticism) discourse. Colonialism and criticism are invariably invoked with reference to the same matrix of cultural structures, psychological assumptions, and in many cases, the same metaphors and linguistic tropes. Traditional accounts of the Irish literary tradition and its relationship with the struggle for political liberation are misplaced, therefore, if they offer to analyse the one (colonial) formation without also bringing the same deconstructive techniques to bear on the other (cultural) discourse – the discourse on which colonialism traditionally depended for the dissemination of its hegemony, and through which post-colonial nations and subjects looked to articulate new histories and new identities. In both instances, one element of an apparently

9

'natural' opposition was traditionally privileged, and in both cases this economy worked by recourse to the same principle of originality, essence, and presence.[4]

I wish now to consider briefly the history of the relationship between these different forms of writing, and to assess the emergence and function of an 'Irish literary tradition'. If, as I am arguing here, such a tradition has no organic validity but is a strategic category constructed in the Irish critical imagination, then there would appear to be serious implications both for Irish cultural history and for contemporary artists and critics.

It is difficult today to conceive of the category of literature without simultaneously conceiving of the category of criticism. One could argue that the artistic function as it has developed in Western civilization seems to imply the critical function, and that art presupposes criticism as built-in element of its practice.[5] On the other hand, it seems clear that contemporary criticism is a highly specialised function occupying specific social and institutional spaces, with specific kinds of individuals performing specific kinds of social and political tasks. Even today, criticism likes to imagine that it fulfils a vital, usually oppositional, role in the production and reproduction of societies, revealing the mechanisms by which texts and authors are linked to their environments, and showing the ways in which cultural forms operate hegemonically to challenge or underpin a given social and political formation.[6] One only has to look at Irish and Irish-related literary criticism of the last two hundred years or so, however, to realise that the radically suspicious role which the discourse claims for itself is not always borne out in fact, and that far from revealing the ways in which power operates in societies, literary criticism can instead create, constitute and conceal the uses and effects of power.

When did the debate over the function of criticism become such an important intellectual issue and, more importantly, why? Again, one can argue that when art becomes aware of itself the critical spirit is born.[7] But literary criticism only begins to become aware of itself, in England and Ireland at least, at a much later time and place in history, a time and place it shares with the age of high imperialism and, curiously enough, with decolonisation. This meta-critical function is, like decolonisation, a relatively new development, and the fact that the two might be genealogically related at some point thus deserves serious attention. One only has to think of some of the names who have engaged in this debate about the function of criticism – Matthew Arnold, Oscar Wilde, W. B. Yeats, T. S. Eliot, F. R. Leavis, and many more – to appreciate not only the intellectual and academic importance of critical discourse but its wider implications for the other well-known issues that preoccupied these writers.[8] At least since the early nineteenth century, the debate surrounding 'the function of criticism', I suggest, has also always been a question of the function of the nation and a question of the relationship between the colonising and the colonised subjects.

Although 'writing about writing' is characterised by diversity of approach and versatility of style, one simple question which can be asked of all secondary or commentative discourse is: 'why criticise?' Within the terms of the tradition where such a question could sensibly and legitimately be asked, there are essentially two answers, emerging from two narratives of the function of criticism *vis-à-vis* the artistic or 'primary' text. The first narrative refers to the functional property of criticism and examines *how* a text creates meaning, while the second refers to criticism's evaluative propensity and looks to see what kinds of writing have been valued by certain historical societies.[9]

The traditional model of critical discourse sees the artistic and the critical acts as ontologically and epistemologically separated, with the artistic text afforded a primary, and the critical a secondary, status. First, runs the argument, we have art and the artist; then we have the handmaiden of art – criticism – the function of which is to describe and explain the primary text, to discover how it operates, the sorts of pleasures it affords and influence it exercises, and then to relate all these findings to another subject. Even Matthew Arnold, who more than any other figure in modern cultural theory is responsible for the rehabilitation of criticism, had to admit 'as a general proposition, that the critical factor is lower than the inventive' and that '[t]he critical power is of lower rank than the creative.'[10] The artistic or creative act precedes the critical act, while criticism, like the parasite it is, feeds off its artistic host, and this is usually offered as an explanation for the inferiority complex suffered by critical discourse in the light of its secondary relationship with the primary text.

Another psychoanalytic metaphor sometimes employed to describe the relationship between literature and criticism is the Oedipus complex, in which the critical text figures as the estranged son desperately trying to suppress its murderous feelings for the artistic text/father. Recourse to such metaphors to describe the power relations between these two forms of writing highlights the structural and conceptual similarities between this cultural discourse and the political relationship between coloniser and colonised; and in as much as the primary/secondary relationship between literature and criticism operates by way of a dialectical system of thought founded on principles of metaphysical presence and absence, it is not inappropriate to discuss its mechanisms and effects in terms of colonisation and resistance, or to attempt to rehabilitate what has traditionally been seen as the lesser partner in the dyad.

This model allows for the two kinds of critical activity mentioned above; it is concerned with the *value* of certain kinds of writing, such value making them different from other kinds of writing (such as criticism) and thus worthy of

11

criticism, while at the same time it is also concerned with *how* these valued texts achieve meaning by virtue of their difference from other kinds of writing (such as criticism). In ancient Greece, for example, Plato valued the kinds of texts which would not influence members of society to acts of imitative evil, while Aristotle attempted to account for the workings of poetic discourse practiced in that society.[11] But it was necessary for Plato to have an understanding of *how* a text may influence people before he could go on to say what was the most valuable kind of writing; conversely, Aristotle must have had an implicit evaluative model if he was to know what kinds of writing in a particular society were worth describing. Plato's concern in *The Republic* was with the health and survival of the state and to this end he evinced a model of criticism which encompassed both evaluation and definition. Even at this early stage of history, criticism was performing unashamed ideological tasks as well as being appointed the moral guardian and social conscience of a certain kind of imagined community. Bad art was to be censored, good art was to be allowed, and the institution of criticism was invented to tell one from the other. Thus, for this traditional model of critical discourse, value and function are seen to be indissolubly linked.

Certain problems arise, however, with this model of literary criticism and its attempts to realise its self-proclaimed revelatory role *vis-à-vis* the primary text. This is because, unlike the criticism which pertains to other cultural forms such as painting and music, literary criticism shares its mode of expression – writing – with its object. As the French literary theorist Gerard Genette writes: 'literary criticism speaks the same language as its object: it is a metalanguage, "discourse upon a discourse." It can therefore be a metaliterature, that is to say, "a literature of which literature itself is the imposed object".'[12] When literary criticism, therefore, attempts to represent something (the meaning of the primary text) it will find itself simultaneously creating something completely different (the critical text), and it thus finds itself having to negotiate a relationship between two, potentially contradictory, systems of representation. The (secondary) critical text must *reveal* the (primary) artistic text's meaning but in so doing it produces another meaning which is specific to itself. But what kind of meaning is it? What status does it have in society? To whom does this meaning belong – the author of the primary text or the critic? If the relationship between the real world and imaginative literature is problematical, then how much more so are the relationships between, first, the 'primary' literary text and the 'secondary' critical text; and second, the critical text and the 'real' world with which the 'primary' text ostensibly deals? And how is criticism to breach this gap between the text being criticised and the critical text being written? Who is to criticise the critics?

Traditional criticism tries to answer all these questions from within its own form, that is, by *constituting* its object at the same time as it purports to *explain* it. The critical text offers to *discover* immanent meaning within the primary text whereas in actual fact, in the words of Roland Barthes, it rather *covers* that text with its own evaluative and prescriptive language.[13] The supposedly secondary text is in fact cast in a specific figural and rhetorical register which does not free or explain the language of the primary text, but overpowers and subverts it. The *value* of a text, therefore, to return to the original criteria, has traditionally been located in the degree to which form and content are in sympathetic alliance, and the purpose of criticism is to explain *how* this alliance occurs.[14]

So, the literary critical text is always embarrassed by the fact that it shares with its master text the same mode of signification, thus possessing potentially the *same* signifying capacity as a discourse it designates as *primary* and *different*. (It is here that the evaluative – 'primary' – and descriptive – 'different' – language of criticism betrays the philosophical and psychological assumptions it shares with colonialist and decolonising discourse). If a certain kind of writing is designated primary, replete, sufficient, intrinsically valuable, then why, going back to the original question, criticise it? The guilty secret known, elided, but always carried by literary criticism is that literature is not so primary or different after all, and that while the critical text must constantly attempt to demonstrate its own unworthiness in the face of its object, it simultaneously deconstructs the terms of that opposition by virtue of the very materiality of its discourse. Far from demonstrating the superior value of the artistic text, criticism merely highlights and stages that text's radical relativity, its inadequacy as a representative of constant, universal meaning, and the fact that art needs commentary, that the primary text depends on the secondary text just as much as literary criticism has traditionally been understood to depend on literature.[15]

At this point, literature's primary status in respect of the critical text is in danger of fracturing under the weight of the contradictions thrown up by the attempt to answer the simple question: why criticise? The whole structure of value and function depends on the simple narrative: first art, then criticism; but this narrative is constantly on the verge of collapse by virtue of the fact that criticism shares its mode of signification with its ostensible object. Critical discourse thus always operates on an alternative and secret agenda, its major preoccupation being not with the (literary) text under scrutiny, but with the (critical) text under construction, not with the author and his or her *representation* of a certain social, political, and historical milieu but with the critic's *construction* of the same. If the gap between these two agendas becomes too wide, breakdown ensues. Etymologically and discursively, therefore, 'criticism' implies crisis. The two words are in fact closely linked, so that whereas 'critical' carries the evaluative and analytic connotations employed here, it also registers, for example, in medical discourse, as something in need of immediate attention, as a crisis.[16]

What are the implications of this ongoing crisis for the study of the role played by culture in Irish decolonisation? What I am suggesting is that when one turns to Irish culture of the past two hundred years or so to observe the emergence of forms of resistance to colonial domination, it is to critical rather than 'imaginative' or 'creative' discourse that one must initially turn. The repeated acts of literature in which the nation is 'performed' throughout the nineteenth and twentieth centuries have themselves to be performed and allowed in a prefiguring critical discourse, a discourse which in its own forms and practices responds to the ongoing narrative of decolonisation. Literature cannot express, reflect, embody – or any other metaphor one chooses – the decolonising nation until it is so constituted by an enabling metadiscourse – literary criticism. The critical act – like the literary or artistic act – is a social act; criticism, like art, is a body of rhetorical strategies waiting to be seized. The history of the specific ways in which Irish critical discourse has been seized as a strategy of Irish decolonisation has, by and large, still to be written.

NOTES

1. Homi Bhabha, ed., *Nation and Narration*, London 1990; Edward Said, *Culture and Imperialism*, London 1993; David Lloyd, *Anomalous States: Irish Writing and the Post-Colonial Moment*, Dublin 1993.

2. The writer most responsible for the general acceptance of the importance of the culture/colonialism nexus is, of course, Edward Said in *Orientalism* (1978) and *Culture and Imperialism* (1993). For the Irish context, see David Lloyd, op. cit., esp. 1–12; Liam O'Dowd, 'Neglecting the Material Dimension: Irish intellectuals and the problem of identity', *The Irish Review*, 3 (1988), 8–17; 'Intellectuals and Political Culture: a unionist-nationalist comparison'; and Eamonn Hughes, ed., *Culture and Politics in Northern Ireland*, Milton Keynes 1991, 151–73, where he writes: '[a]ll the major analyses of modern nationalist movements have detailed the crucial role of intellectuals, especially those of a literary and humanistic orientation' (161). For a coherent dissent-

ing voice, see Simon During, 'Literature – Nationalism's Other? The case for revision', in Bhabha, ed., op. cit., 138–53.

3. Edward Said, *The World, The Text and The Critic*, New York 1983, 53.

4. As the language here shows, my reasoning on this matter has been coloured by Derrida and his work on what he calls the 'logic of supplementarity', which, in the words of one of his commentators, 'is precisely this strange reversal of values whereby an apparently derivative or secondary term takes on the crucial role in determining an entire structure of assumptions'. See Christopher Norris, *Derrida*, London 1987, 67.

5. This is the position argued by Paul de Man in *Blindness and Insight: Essays in the rhetoric of contemporary criticism*, London 1983, *passim*.

6. This model of critical discourse, emerging out of the Kantian and Marxist philosophical traditions, is most closely associated with both generations of the Frankfurt School (see, for example, Theodor Adorno, trans. S. and S. Weber, 'Cultural Criticism and Society', in *Prisms*, Cambridge, Mass. 1967, 19–34); but it emerges in much of the contemporary neo-Arnoldian debate about the 'function of criticism'. See Tony Bennett, *Outside Literature*, London 1990; Terry Eagleton, *Literary Criticism: An Introduction*, Oxford 1983; Frank Lentricchia, *Criticism and Social Change*, Chicago 1983; Said 1983, op. cit.

7. See Michel Foucault, *The Order of Things: An archaeology of the human sciences*, London 1970, 78–81.

8. See Matthew Arnold, *The Study of Celtic Literature*, London 1900; Oscar Wilde, 'The Critic as Artist' (1891), in *Intentions and The Soul of Man*, London 1969, 99–224; W. B. Yeats, *Essays and Introductions*, London 1961; T. S. Eliot, *On Poetry and Poets*, London 1957; F. R. Leavis, *Revaluation: Tradition and Development in English Poetry*, London 1936.

9. This bifurcation of metadiscursive activity emerges in similar ways in classical and Christian discourse, organised around an historical split which develops between a primary sacred text replete with immanent meaning, requiring commentary, and a primary secular text which looks to intervene into meaning, requiring criticism. See Foucault 1970, and de Man 1983, op. cits.

10. Matthew Arnold, 'The Function of Criticism at the Present Time' (1865), in M. H. Abrams, *et al, The Norton Anthology of English Literature*, New York 1979, 1405–6.

11. Plato, trans. A. D. Lindsay, *The Republic*, London 1976; Aristotle, trans. J. Warrington, *Poetics*, London 1975. For a reading of Plato's attempt to prop up a philosophical structure based the difference between 'good' and 'bad' writing, and its implications for the history of philosophy, see Derrida, trans. B. Johnson, *Dissemination*, Chicago 1981, 61–171.

12. Gerard Genette, 'Structuralism and Literary Criticism', in David Lodge, ed., *Modern Criticism and Theory: A Reader*, Harlow 1988, 63.

13. Roland Barthes, 'Criticism as Language', in David Lodge, ed., *20th Century Literary Criticism*, Harlow 1972, 650.

14. See John Barrell, *Poetry, Language and Politics*, Manchester 1988, 1–17, for a brilliant analysis of the way in which this evaluative/descriptive model has influenced the emergence of critical discourse in relation to English poetry.

15. For all their supposed differences, Foucault and Derrida share a similar line on the concept of commentary or criticism. In 'The Order of Discourse' (in Robert Young, ed., *Untying the Text*, London 1981, 48–78), Foucault writes: '[b]y a paradox which it always displaces but never escapes, the commentary must say for the first time what had, nonetheless, already been said, and must tirelessly repeat what had, however, never been said ... it allows us to say something other than the text itself, but on condition that it is this text itself which is said, and in a sense *completed* ... The commentary-principle limits the chance element in discourse by the

play of an identity which would take the form of repetition and sameness' (58–9, my italics). This accords with Derrida's approach (in *Of Grammatology*, Baltimore 1976), where he traces through the paradoxical relationship between sign (or literature) and supplement (or criticism) – supplement in the sense of something extra *and* in the sense of making complete: '[y]et if reading must not be content with doubling the text, it cannot legitimately transgress the text towards something other than it, towards a referent (a reality that is metaphysical, historical, psychobiographical, etc.) Or towards a signified outside the text whose content could take place, could have taken place outside of language, that is to say, in the sense that we give the word here, outside of writing in general' (158). For a comparison of these seminal modern thinkers, see Said 1983, op. cit., 178–225.

16.   See Raymond Williams, *Keywords*, London 1984, 84–6, for the historical links between 'criticism', 'critical', and 'crisis'. Many other writers have noted these links: de Man, op cit.; Chris Baldick, *The Social Mission of English Criticism 1848–1932*, Oxford 1983; W. E. Cain, *The Crisis in Criticism: Theory, literature, and reform in English studies*, Baltimore and London 1984.

3

Constructing the contemporary self: the works of Iain Banks

Tim Middleton

Iain Banks has written twelve novels, comprising seven 'mainstream' texts and five science fictions, and a collection of short stories.[1] All of these have been produced since 1984 and yet, despite this fairly prodigious output, Banks's work has tended – the *Granta* 'Best of Young British Novelists' excepted – to be neglected by academic critics. Whilst his mainstream fictions are generally reviewed in the 'quality' press, the coverage tends to be based around laments over his use of the codes of popular genres like science fiction, horror and the thriller. For example, Natasha Walter's review of *The Crow Road* (1992), complains that the novel's 'detective' story plot-line tends to detract from the 'rites of passage narrative' and as such represents 'padding' which 'muffles the occasional pure notes'.[2] Overall, the reviews of Bank's works in the press balance laments about his tendency to 'slum it' by using devices and motifs from popular genres with more general complaints about his literary short-comings.[3] Most reviewers however do have some positive points to make, often in terms of praise for his ability to keep the reader involved. Nicholas Lezard's recent review of *Complicity* strikes several of these notes: 'Iain Banks is no great writer. His characters clank, the dialogue is crude, the *grand guignol* scenes mechanically contrived. And yet this is not the first Banks novel I stayed up half the night to finish: he is a great plotter, and, morally, very acute.'[4]

This essay is an attempt to begin to counter what I see as the unwarranted neglect and the ongoing disparagement of Banks's fiction by offering some suggestions about the relevance of his work to debates about contemporary writing and subjectivity. This essay also seeks to rework existing critical conceptions of Scottishness in relation to the characteristic patterns of Banks's fiction, and also to draw out the connections between notions of pluralistic identity and recent theoretical work on the construction of the subject.

Iain Banks's fictions may be characterised by the way in which they repeatedly centre themselves upon the complex locus of desires, needs, and hopes that we might gloss as constitutive of a subjectivity. In Banks's fiction the subject's desires, needs, and hopes are always already channelled, thwarted and/or compromised by the symbolic order of the culture in which the individual is situated. In his 'mainstream' fiction he often probes the interrelation of self and society by removing central characters from the real and its mundanities and placing them in extremis: exile, or at least isolation. Thus we have Frank in *The Wasp Factory* (1984) living on an island, playing his own dangerous and destructive games; a coma victim's unconscious fantasies played alongside recollections of his rise to wealth in 1970s and '80s Edinburgh in *The Bridge* (1986): the fugitive self of the retired rock star in *Espedair Street* (1987) who lives in a disused church and hides from the community which socialised him by pretending to be the caretaker rather than the building's eccentric owner.

In what follows I begin with a brief outline of Scottishness before moving on to suggest ways in which this might be reworked when linked to ideas derived from recent postmodern theory, particularly the work of Jean Baudrillard. The essay concludes with a brief reading of Banks's 1986 novel *The Bridge* in relation to these ideas but also draws upon Lacanian theory in its account of the construction of subjectivity suggested by that novel.

Scottishness is something of a problematic term in critical debates about Scotland's literature. Many of the debates about writing and national identity raised by Hugh MacDiarmid, Edwin Muir and others in relation to the writing of the 1920s and '30s are being turned to by critics seeking to account for the recent developments in Scottish literature.[5] As many commentators have argued, the boom in Scottish writing since the 1970s may in part be attributed to the cultural phenomenon of an increasingly antagonistic dialogism with that bellicose and ruthlessly self-serving version of Englishness peddled through Thatcherism which was a feature of Scottish experience from the late 1970s to the recent past. As Gavin Wallace puts it: 'there is a sense in which Scottish fiction prospers in inverse proportion to the difficulties of the cultural and political situation which confronts it.'[6] In the programme for the Scottish TUC's 'Day for Scotland', Pat Kane writes of the 1980s as a period of identity crisis; a crisis which has gradually been assuaged by the development of what he sees as a newly sophisticated Scottishness: 'a truly modern Scottish consciousness: more confident, flexible and diverse than ever before.'[7] For Kane this is part and parcel of the ongoing development of what he terms 'a plural and principled national identity'.[8] Interestingly, this emphasis on pluralism might be seen as a contemporary version of Gregory Smith's concept of the 'Caledonian antisyzygy'.[9]

According to Smith, Scottish literature was to be characterised by its diversity and pluralism. It is, he wrote, 'remarkably varied', and he went on to suggest that 'perhaps in the very combination of opposites ... we have a reflection of the contrast which the Scot shows at every turn'.[10] For Smith, antisyzygy was to be seen in what he saw as the characteristic yoking together of realism with fantasy in Scottish textual practice: as he puts it:

> the Scottish muse has ... loved reality, sometimes to maudlin affection for the commonplace, [but] she has loved not less the airier pleasures to be found in the confusion of the senses, in the fun of things thrown topsy-turvy, in the horns of elf-land and the voices of the mountain.[11]

For Smith, the real and the fantastic are 'the polar twins of the Scottish muse', habitually yoked together into the 'Caledonian antisyzygy'.[12] Whilst there have been some recent attempts to assess the relevance of Smith's notion for contemporary Scottish fiction, the term's links with notions pertaining to the anomalous nature of postmodernity have not been fully explored.[13] The term antisyzygy both attracted me as a convenient gloss on the divided selves and mixed genres of Banks's fiction but also puzzled me partly because it seemed, on further investigation, to be somewhat tautological.[14]

Syzygy means the pairing and yoking together of opposites; but a pairing in which the two opposed terms or things retain distinctiveness; as in, the *OED* suggests, copulation. Syzygy in its astrological sense refers to the pairing of opposites by an observer and even in its biological sense refers to a state in which two organisms co-exist in the same organic structure.[15] Thus it concerns opposition and conjunction; difference and similarity brought together into a yoked unity but always remaining distinct. Antisyzygy must be the opposite of syzygy – meaning not yoked; not paired; not opposed; or perhaps meaning a yoking in which things actually do merge and meld; in which distinctiveness and identity are lost. To be antisyzygentic, in the sense which arises from the *OED*'s definition of syzygy, would mean to be wholly homogenous; undifferentiated and always identical which is surely not what Smith had in mind. As a basis for textual practice, antisyzygy would, it seems to me, be deadly dull: Bakhtin's monoglossia with knobs on.

If one stresses the idea that antisyzygy means 'not yoked', then one might justifiably claim that it meant *insisting* on autonomy; at a political level this might be seen as a crucial part of Scottishness but for individuals (as opposed to nations) to be autonomous to this extent implies either the morbid self-absorption of a quasi-autistic state or at least a John Majorish lack of distinctiveness. At the level of textual practice, then, I would suggest that antisyzygy as described by Smith is closer to what the *OED* defines as syzygy. Syzygy strikes me as potentially much more interesting than antisyzygy, both as a characteristic of textuality but also as a way of conceiving subjectivity. In its stress on structures and phenomena that present similarities and differences simultaneously it has much in common with notions of the subject suggested by theorists of postmodernity.

Much work has been done in critical and social theory that supports a characterisation of the contemporary subject as caught in what for Baudrillard is the characteristically postmodern condition of anomaly; a state which has particular resonances with the notion of syzygy. Baudrillard's fractal stage centres upon versions of self which are in flux: he conceives of the subject as a locus for a 'fractal multiplication of body images': a space or site in which an individual combines any number of identities.[16] For Baudrillard, the fractal stage of postmodernity generates 'a play with all of the forms of identity',[17] and occasions that he dubs 'the time of transvestism' in which the subject and the role they occupy are subtly distinct. Thus a performative quality is brought to all human acts, and here one might make connections with the (somewhat more cogently argued) work of Judith Butler on postmodern identity and gender. In Butler's work, the subject's ability to bring an element of performativity to the projection and establishment of gendered identity produces a situation in which identity is fluid and not immutable, and is, in part, syzygetic. Butler argues that the subject constructs a gendered identity through 'the repetition of oppressive and painful gender norms'.[18] Performative gender identities are not, therefore, signs of an individual's freedom but rather, as Butler puts it, a way of working 'the trap that one is inevitably in'.

Butler's work supports the notion that constructing identity is a kind of textual practice: it has clear links with the well-established notion that the subject is constructed by discourse even as s/he uses discourse to encode a particular identity.[19] The fluidity of identity described above provides a starting point from which to develop the notion of syzygy as a fundamental aspect of contemporary textual practice and constructions of identity. I will attempt to work with some of these ideas in an outline analysis of the construction of the subject in Banks's 1986 novel *The Bridge*.

In an interview, Banks declared *The Bridge* to be 'the best of the bunch in terms of the actual craft of the novel'.[20] The text tells two ultimately inter-linked stories: one, a fantasy concerning a Mr Orr which takes up three of the book's seven sections and is divided into three substantial sequences (Metaphormosis, Metaorpheus and Metamorphosis), which recount the fantastical story of Mr Orr's experiences whilst living in and investigating a Kafkaesque community spread along a gigantic version of what turns out to be the Forth Rail Bridge. Mr Orr's story is framed by four sections (Coma, Triassic, Eocene and Coda) which tell of the rise to power of a Scottish business man called Lennox, from the late teens in the mid-1960s to his successful if unhappy life as an Edinburgh yuppie in the mid-1980s.[21]

Each section of his realist narrative commences with Lennox's thoughts as he lies in a coma following a car crash on the Forth Road Bridge: as the titles of the three Orr-related sections imply, the novel is concerned with various processes of crossing over and transition: metaphormosis suggests a process based upon correspondences; the idea of 'carrying from one place to another' seems relevant to this novel of bridging, as does the notion that what we have is a description of one thing (Lennox's life) in terms of another (Orr's experiences on the bridge). These connections are implied rather than stated, thus the text is very much in the syzygetic mould: it contains the two narratives and there is conjunction at numerous points but the stories remain distinct.[22]

Mr Orr's story is a projection of Lennox's dystopic fantasies; indeed there seems to be some kind of compulsion at work in relation to Lennox's involvement with the activities of his alter-ego. Many of the realist sections begin with the narrating Lennox's discourse being interrupted by fragments of the Orr-related narrative which is to follow, and often we encounter Lennox resisting the commencement of Orr's narrative. This happens, for example, right at the start of the novel. At the end of the 'Coma' sequence we read:

> [m]aybe all the rest was a dream (yeah, sure), and I wake up to ('Thedarkstation') – what was that? Did you hear that? Did I hear that? *The dark station*. There it was again. A noise like a train whistle; something about to depart. Something about to begin, or end, or both. Something that is THE DARK STATION me, Or not (me no know. Me new here. No ask me). *The dark station*. Oh, all right.[23]

It comes as something of a surprise on a first reading of the novel when we turn the page to begin the first section of 'Metaphormosis' to find that the chapter commences with the words, '[t]he dark station, shuttered and empty, echoed to the distant, fading whistle of the departing train' (17). As the novel unfolds we are forced to read the fantasy tale of Orr's life on the Bridge in the light of Lennox's rise to power in 1970s and '80s Scotland: the parallels are too great to overlook. By the final section of the novel, Lennox is making the connection with the Orr narrative clear for the reading: he is now out of the coma but initially reluctant to re-enter reality:

> Oh God, back to Thatcher's Britain and Reagan's world, back to all the usual bullshit. At least the bridge was predictable in its oddness, at least it was comparatively *safe*.
>
> Well, maybe not, I don't know. I know one thing ... The choice is not between dream and reality; it is between two different dreams. One is my

own; the bridge and all I made of it. The other is our collective dream, our corporate imagery. We live the dream; call it American, call it Western, call it Northern or call it just that of all we humans, all life. I was part of one dream, for good or ill, and it was half nightmare and I almost let it kill me, but it hasn't. Yet, anyway.

What's changed?

Not the dream, not the result of our dreams which we call the world, not our hi-tech life. Me, then? Maybe. Who knows; could be anything, inside here. Just won't be able to tell until I get back out again, and start living the shared dream, abandoning my own (283).

Lennox's alertness to the problematic of reality and his desire to remain in the relatively safe confines of his coma both locates him as occupying a characteristically anomalous position *vis-à-vis* reality but also defines him as a quintessentially postmodern subject forced to choose between identities. The novel insists upon the divided yet linked (syzygetic) nature of the selves which individuals don in their many-sided negotiations with the culture in which they find themselves.[24] This spills over into a subject's fantasy life because once under the yoke of the symbolic order even the projections of fantasy are based upon misrecognition: thus Orr repeats the contradictions and crises which Lennox experiences in reality.[25] Syzygy is also evident in the novel's formal organisation, both in terms of the linked yet distinct narratives of Orr and Lennox and, more generally, in the crucial role of intertextuality (in the fullest sense of the term). The novel draws upon diverse 'external' signifying systems such as the politics of the 1979 devolution referendum, 1980s new wave music, Claude Chabrol's 1971 film *The Butcher,* and the Orpheus myth. The text's use of the Orpheus myth is particularly interesting in relation to my concerns with subjectivity, in that it foregrounds the separation of mind and body.

In *The Bridge* there are a number of direct links with the Orpheus myth: in part, the character Orr might be seen as an Orpheus figure in that he appears on the bridge world following a loss; there is also the title of section 4, Metaorpheus; in Chapter 2 of Metaphormosis, Orr's faked dream of a sea battle is described in a way in which might be seen as a link to Orpheus's adventures with the Argonauts; more directly, in Chapter 3 of the Metaorpheus section, Orr's dream of a being trapped on a bridge from which he watches the orgiastic rituals of a group of women could be seen as an echo of Orpheus and the Maenads, as can Chapter 4 of this section which tells of a descent into the underworld.

The double loss of Orpheus is something which has inspired a number of writers and theorists. As Lacan argues, 'we have, in Eurydice twice lost, the

23

most potent image we can find of the relation between Orpheus the analyst and the unconscious.'[26] The separation of soul and body foregrounded in the Orpheus myth provides a metaphor for the separation of conscious and unconscious, for the loss of the imaginary contingent upon accessing the real via the symbolic order of language. The Lacanian account of subjectivity foregrounds the role of the social in constructing the psychological; the Lacanian subject is a site of contested and unstable meanings arising from the yoking together of the Real and the Imaginary by the Symbolic.

As David Fisher notes in *Cultural Theory and Psychoanalytic Tradition*, for Lacan the 'deepest needs and impulses of the individual are products of, formed and deformed by' the society in which we find ourselves.[27] However, in Lacan's work the constructed self is always based upon *méconnaissance*, on misrecognition.[28] The mirror stage is an illusion, a reflection misread, there is no wholeness, no control; as such it could be read as part of the elaborate con-trick which the ego (as agency of the Symbolic) plays upon us. To become a self – in the Lacanian scheme of things – you have to objectify yourself through the process of mis-identification associated with the entry into a culture's symbolic order: you objectify yourself as an 'I' but in doing so cast off the rich possibilities of the imaginary and subject yourself to the codes of the Symbolic. The Lacanian subject is founded and founders upon a radical splitting of the self: a *spaltung* which is to the fore in *The Bridge*.

The Lacanian subject has a distorted sense of self: it is built upon a lack associated with the casting-off of fantasy. An anxiety regarding fantasy is very much part of the character of Lennox in the novel – at one point he argues strongly for adherence to rationality, claiming that 'that's the only way to understand anything. First, *does it work?* Then, *how?*' (109). As the narrator points out, this stems from Lennox's belief in:

> a sort of Unified Field Theory of consciousness; it was there to be under-stood, emotions and feelings and logical thought together; a whole, an entity however disparate ... it would all eventually be comprehended; it was just a matter of time, and research. It seemed so obvious to him that he had great difficulty understanding anybody else's point of view. (*ibid.*)

Thus Lennox's characterisation bears out Lacan's account of the ego as 'the realm of deep resistance, the repository of absence, incompleteness and spurious knowledge'.[29] In practice, this means that the 'ego' is a limiting socially-derived constraint placed upon the self, and *The Bridge* works to suggest the ways in which Lennox's socialisation and the contradictions of the culture in which he finds himself create his sense of self. In this he is like many of the central characters in Banks's fictions from *The Wasp Factory* to *The Crow Road* and *Complicity*. All are depicted as having to mediate between inner desires and the constraints of the social and as such are engaged upon the essentially familiar – in Freud's sense of the uncanny – activity of negotiating the anomalies arising from the syzygetic nature of contemporary culture.[30]

NOTES

1. Mainstream: *The Wasp Factory* (1984), *Walking on Glass* (1985), *The Bridge* (1986), *Espedair Street* (1987), *Canal Dreams* (1989), *The Crow Road* (1992), *Complicity* (1993). Science Fiction: *Consider Phlebas* (1987), *The State of the Art* (1991) *The Player of Games* (1991), *Use of Weapons* (1991) *Against a Dark Background* (1993), *Feersum Endjinn* (1994).

2. 'Growing Up in the Glens', *The Times Literary Supplement*, April 17th 1992, 21.

3. I am deeply indebted to the very helpful publicity staff of Banks's publishers, Little, Brown & Co., for supplying me with a clippings pack of review material relating to his more recent texts.

4. *The Guardian*, 'Paperbacks: Round up', 14th June 1994.

5. See, for example, Manfred Maizahn's *Aspects of Identity: The contemporary Scottish novel (1978–1981) as national self-expression*, Frankfurt 1984. Also see Peter Zenzinger, 'Contemporary Scottish Fiction', in *Scotland: Literature, culture, politics*, Heidelberg 1989, 215–39.

6. Gavin Wallace and Randall Stevenson, eds., *The Scottish Novel since the Seventies*, Edinburgh 1993, 2. This point is supported by James Robertson in his helpful article, 'Scottish Publishing: Balancing the books for the '90s', *Radical Scotland*, 50 (April/May 1991), 29–31.

7. Pat Kane, 'A Day for Scotland', *Radical Scotland*, 46 (August/September 1990), 15. (Reprinted from the programme of the STUC's 'Day for Scotland', July 14th 1990.)

8. ibid.

9. See G. Gregory Smith, *Scottish Literature: Character and influence*, London 1919, esp. 1–40. The concept has been cogently summarised by Robert Crawford in his argument that 'the Cal. Ant. idea was that Scottish culture (especially literature) produced energy by bringing together clashing opposites', 'Going for the Burns: Edinburgh Arts Festival', *The Sunday Times*, 15th August 1993, 9–12. Also see Edwin Muir's discussion in *Scott and Scotland*, London 1936, 91–114.

10. Smith, op. cit., 4.

11. ibid., 19.

12. ibid., 20.

13. Manfred Malzahn, op. cit., seeks to reassess the relevance of Smith's notion to contemporary Scottish fiction.

14. Thom Nairn makes a similar point regarding Banks's work's affinity to Smith's concept in his article, 'Iain Banks and the Fiction Factory', in *The Scottish Novel since the Seventies*, 129.

15. As in a diplozoon in which the creature is made up of a number of zoolds — as in the various 'persons' making up a colonial animal (*OED*).

16. See Baudrillard's essays on 'Transaesthetics', 'Transexuality' and 'Transeconomics', in *The Transparency of Evil: Essays on extreme phenomena*, trans. James Benedict, London 1993. For helpful commentary on these, see Best and Kellner's discussion of Baudrillard's work in *Postmodern Theory*, London 1991, esp. 126–45.

17. Best and Kellner, op. cit., 137.

18. See Butler, *Gender Trouble: Feminism and the subversion of identity*, New York and London 1990, and *Bodies that Matter: On the discursive limits of 'sex'*, New York and London 1993. I quote

from the helpfully concise account of some of the ideas raised in *Gender Trouble* provided by Butler's comments in interview with Liz Kotz, *Artforum: International*, November 1992, 84.

19. There are interesting connections to be made here with the Bakhtin/Vološinov-inspired work of Jerome Bruner on what he terms 'transactional contextualism', which posits that a textual practice is always a re-deployment of a culture's 'contexts of practice'; sources for meaning which are brought to bear on our practices as human agents at a given time and place. See Bruner, *Actual Minds: Possible worlds*, Cambridge, Mass. 1986, 57–69.

20. Interview with Banks by James Robertson, 'Bridging Styles: A conversation with Iain Banks', *Radical Scotland*, 42 (December 1989/January 1990), 26-7.

21. Thom Nairn offers a cogent reading of Lennox's Scottishness in his article on Banks in *The Scottish Novel Since the Seventies*. See also Peter Zenzinger's brief comments on the novel in 'Contemporary Scottish Fiction', op. cit., 231.

22. Connections between the world of the Bridge and the world of Lennox abound: they include the fact that Orr's girlfriend gives him a monogrammed handkerchief and Lennox's gives him a monogrammed scarf, and also (at another level) the fact that Orr's girlfriend on the Bridge, Abberlaine, is actually the name of one of Lennox's nurses, and that Orr's psychiatrist Dr Joyce has the same name as Lennox's consultant.

23. *The Bridge*, Abacus, London 1990, 12–13. Further quotations are from this edition and attributed in the text.

24. I am drawing here upon the work of V. N. Vološinov, in particular his concept of 'inner speech' as a product of the subject's 'many sided interaction with his milieu' ('Discourse in Life: Discourse in poetry', in A. Shukman, ed., *Bakhtin School Papers*, Oxford 1983, 26–7). Also see *Marxism and the Philosophy of Language*, London and New York 1973.

25. The Abberlaine/Andrea character, for example: also see note 22, above.

26. Jacques Lacan, trans. Alan Sheridan, *The Four Fundamental Concepts of Psychoanalysis*, Harmondsworth 1979, 25.

27. David Fisher, *Cultural Theory and the Psychoanalytic Tradition*, New Brunswick and London 1991, 5.

28. I use the term 'constructed self' rather than 'ego' as I am working with a (broadly) phenomenological frame of reference in which the subject is constructed by a culture through discourse and its associated iconography. The ego is only part of the subject, but is that which has been modified by the direct influence of the external world. See Sigmund Freud, 'The Ego and the Id' (1923), *The Essentials of Psychoanalysis*, Harmondsworth 1986, 439–83.

29. Fisher, op. cit., 8.

30. On the notion of the anomalous as the defining characteristic of postmodernity see, for example, Jean Baudrillard, trans. P. Beitchman and W. G. Niesluchowski, *Fatal Strategies*, New York and London 1990, 25–70. Freud's argument that the uncanny is dependent upon the sense that 'in reality nothing is new or alien, but something familiar and old-established in the mind that has become alienated from it only through the process of repression', also has links with the notions of syzygetic identity that this essay has sought to explore ('The Uncanny', *Standard Edition*, Volume 17, 241).

Derek Walcott: voicing whose identity?

Michael Parker

                                                          Each
Will be barren of ancestral memory
But each endowed richly with such emptiness
From which to dream, surmise, invent, immortalise.[1]

Heteroglossia has been a feature of Derek Walcott's writing from the outset, in part as a conscious challenge to the monologic discourse of imperialism. Like the work of many other post-colonial writers, Walcott's poetry bears the marks of a complex, plural linguistic inheritance through which he has attempted to reflect and re-present 'the multifarious tensions of his own culture'.[2] For Walcott, the Caribbean writer can serve the community by acting as a 'filter and purifier, never losing the tone and strength of common speech as he uses the hieroglyphs, symbols or alphabet of the official one.'[3] Having, like the central character of Jean Rhys's *Wide Sargasso Sea*, endured a kind of internal exile as a child, separated from the white colonists by his colour, and from the black community by colour, class, religion and language – whereas most St. Lucians spoke French Creole, Walcott's family used English as their everyday language – Walcott has transmuted that continuing sense of exile and division into art.

The poet's enterprise, and indeed that of post-colonial literatures in general, has been the 'forging of a language that went beyond mimicry, a dialect which had the force of revelation as it invented names for things, one which finally settled on its own mode of inflection.'[4] That image of 'forging' inevitably invites comparisons with James Joyce, an entirely appropriate role model for Walcott. (Indeed, in *Omeros*, Walcott actually names Joyce as 'our age's Omeros').[5] One recalls Stephen Daedalus's announced mission at the end of *A Portrait of the Artist as a Young Man*, 'to forge in the smithy of my soul the uncreated consciousness of my race.' The voice of Joyce surfaces again in *Another Life*, when the narrator remembers a:

plaster-of-Paris Venus, which
his yearning had made marble, half-cracked
unsilvering mirror of black servants[6]

This is an image which brings to mind Stephen's telling comparison of Irish art with 'the cracked lookingglass of a servant' in *Ulysses*.[7] For much of this century, the endeavour of post-colonial writers has been to forge such a language, to create reflections in its 'half-cracked' mirror, to achieve a sense of cultural affirmation by occupying the occupiers' language, and making it fit to their own purposes, and by refusing to be fixed solely as victims of history.

The most obvious examples of Walcott's skill as an orchestrator of many voices are in 'The Schooner *Flight*' and in *Omeros*. Instead, however, I would like to focus on a number of less well-known lyrics. In *Another Life* (1973), Walcott speaks of his passionate, unfulfilled desire to capture in paint 'the paradoxical flash of an instant/in which every facet was caught/in a crystal of ambiguities'[8] and his later recognition that his was a 'different gift/its element metaphor', the brilliant indeterminacy of words. Much of the brilliance in Walcott's writing is derived from its lyric force, its playing with voices, its multi-faceted cultural awarenesses. This is evident from his earliest poems. 'Prelude' (1948), the opening poem from *Collected Poems*, employs a constant shifting of perspective within and between the narrating voice and the imagined 'blue' eyed perceptions of the tourists sailing by, between the local and the larger world and its expectations. The narrator observes:'[t]he variegated fists of cloud that gather over/the uncouth features of this, my prone island',[9] but does so 'with legs crossed along the daylight', at ease with himself seemingly despite climatic and imperial threat. This threat comes also in the form of 'tourist booklets, ardent binoculars' which attempt to construct the islanders in their texts as 'happy' in their idyllic ignorance, contented in their 'uncouth', 'prone' position. The ease is illusory – as it so frequently is in a Walcott poem – since the colonial presence constrains not just political life, but also poetic discourse, which it seeks to regiment. The speaker laments the constant need to '[s]traigh-ten my tie', and the fact that his life 'must not be made public/Until I have learnt to suffer/In accurate iambics,[10] though in fact the rigorous disciplines of verse form and rhyme are ones which he has come to relish. In another early piece, 'Origins', although one finds at its outset echoes of Dylan Thomas in the shock of its images and playing with extremes: '[t]he flowering breaker deton-ates the surf/White bees hiss in the coral skull', as the poem progresses the focus shifts inward, moving within the consciousness of a Caribbean/Caliban self, who is '[n]ameless ... among olives of algae', in contrast to the named classical heroes – Hector, Achilles, Aeneas, Ulysses.[11] Walcott reaches back past the colonial era and its literature to a classical and pre-classical, hybrid point of origin and authority, a 'Greek and African pantheon', in search of validation through the power to name, instead of being named: '[t]he mind, among sea-wrack, sees its mythopoeic coast/Seeks, like the polyp, to take root in itself'.[12]

The poem's dialogic brings together Egypt, Greece, Guinea, the Caribbean, 'stitching two worlds', like '[t]he retching hulks of caravels', which sewed together Europe, Africa and the Americas in their sickening trade. Walcott's ambition to 'purify the language of the tribe', to 'use my hand' to give 'voice to one people's grief', to quote Shabine in 'The Schooner *Flight*', is signalled in parts IV, V, VI, and VII, with the significant semantic shift away from 'I' to 'We' and 'Our'.[13] 'Origins', like Seamus Heaney's poem 'Gifts of Rain', celebrates forbears and their forbearance, nets their lost voices, and offers rites of atonement to:

[t]hose whose back on hillsides buckles on the wind
To sow the grain of Guinea in the mouths of the dead,
Who, hurling their bone-needled nets over the cave mouth,
Harvest ancestral voices from its surf ...
Whose sweat, touching earth, multiplies in crystals of sugar.[14]

'A Far Cry from Africa' similarly stitches the Africa of the present to the pre-colonial African past, to assert the past's contemporaneity, and illustrates effectively the difficulties some black writers have had in what Susan Willis has called 'reversing the maps of domination':

[w]hile we in the First World are apt to conceive of the Caribbean as a hodge-podge of discrete islands, the poets see it as a whole, often referring to it as a basin, a cradle or a trough, held in place by a dynamic relationship to the Americas and Africa.[15]

The opening line – '[a] wind is ruffling the tawny pelt/Of Africa' – contains perhaps an ironic echo of Harold Macmillan's famous speech of 3rd February 1960 to the South African Parliament about 'the winds of change' blowing across Africa. However, some seven weeks later, on 21st March, when a crowd at Sharpeville gathered to demonstrate against the compulsory carrying of identity cards as part of the apartheid laws, police opened fire on them, killing seventy and wounding over a hundred more. Walcott specifically names this event in *Dream on Monkey Mountain*, where the Corporal exults as he takes down his rifle:

[t]here's nothing quite so exciting as putting down the natives ... Let them run ahead. Then I'll have good reason for shooting them down. Sharpeville? Attempting to escape. Attempting to escape. Attempting to escape the prison of their lives. That's the most dangerous crime.[16]

Though its first verse specifically alludes to events in Kenya, the poem clearly embraces the whole continent and beyond, and the 'nervous condition' of the colonised everywhere. 'What's happened to my mind?' asks the Corporal at one point in *Dream of Monkey Mountain.* 'It was never yours',[17] comes the reply; '[t]hey can't choose; they must have both. Two worlds; that makes two bewitchings ... each day the split widens. The status of 'native' is a nervous condition introduced and maintained by the settler among colonised people *with their consent.*'[18]

'A Far Cry from Africa' reflects Walcott's own divisions and the ambivalence of black liberal humanists in their response to the confrontation in the late 1950s to early 1960s between British colonial forces and the Mau-Mau in Kenya, a struggle which is not only physical and political, but ideological. The poem is a text about texts and readings. It dramatises an attempt to turn towards and from, to take up a position, only to find itself caught by contradictory awarenesses – the competing voices of John Donne's humanist compassion and Frantz Fanon's legitimate outrage. Black Africa is represented initially as a graceful animal, with a 'tawny pelt', but occupied by parasites. At first it seems that the reductive image of the Kikuyu – 'quick as flies' battening on 'the bloodstreams' – fixes them as the source of the disease, but then the last word of the line – 'veldt' – reminds us of the political and linguistic dispossession which has given rise to the carnage. Though the text appears to be setting up an equal hierarchy between white and black, and offering equal condemnation, I would suggest that in fact violence by and upon the blacks is always and appropriately placed in its colonial context. The colonial powers were living through what Sartre terms 'the moment of the boomerang', when the violence that colonialism launched came back to strike its beneficiaries.[19]

> Statistics justify and scholars seize
> The salients of colonial policy.
> What is that to the white child hacked in bed?
> To savages, expendable as Jews?[20]

The depersonalising monologic forces of the imperial power – which elevates number ('statistics') over individual human rights, which prefers justification to justice, which uses education as a tool of cultural violence ('scholars seize') as well as military measures ('salients') – have caused the appalling murder of 'the white child hacked in bed'. But before the reader – white or black – is allowed time to be overwhelmed or appalled by horror and anger at that singular individual atrocity, the poem ironically reminds them of the 'superior' scale of slaughter of which 'civilised' Europeans have proved themselves capable.

('Progress is history's dirty joke', Shabine says in 'The Schooner *Flight*'.)[21] Having fixed the 'Other' as 'savages', as Conrad does so often in *Heart of Darkness*, Eurocentric ideology then sets about 'proving' their expendability. Walcott challenges what Said calls the 'rigidly binomial oppositions' of 'ours' and 'theirs', so beloved of and so marked in colonial discourse.[22] The reference to 'Jews' directly invites comparisons to be made between the Jewish holocaust and the diaspora which preceded it, and that suffered by the enslaved native populations of Africa and America, and reminds one that Nazism, as John Carey has shown, merely embodies European racist attitudes carried to their savagely logical conclusions: '[t]he tragedy of *Mein Kampf* is that it was not, in many respects, a deviant work but one firmly rooted in European intellectual orthodoxy.'[23]

After twenty-three lines of third-person narration invoking shifting ideological positions on Africa and the Africans – as violated paradise, cradle of civilization and killing field – the narrating voice openly acknowledges its inner divisions. The speaker confesses to being genetically, culturally and linguistically 'divided to the vein', in love, like Yeats, with 'the English tongue', but impassionedly at odds with British power and policy. The cry in the final line – 'How can I turn from Africa and live?' – is perhaps representative of many thousands of black voices in America and the Caribbean – striving to forgive, determined to remember and resist – determinedly defining itself by invoking its lost point of origin. Gerald Moore asks the question, 'Is Africa somehow an obstacle to living, or a necessary condition of it?'[24] 'Africa' stands to Walcott perhaps like the problematical 'stone in the living stream' to Yeats in 'Easter 1916'. Though the title, 'A Far Cry from Africa', suggests distance, the poem itself is a deeply engaged one.

The critical importance of intertextual voices to Walcott may be further illustrated in 'The Castaway', which begins in a particular local parish complete with palms, mangroves, exotic flora, but then opens out into a larger, universal landscape, a Beckett-like world without a transcendental signified, perhaps in no small part affected by the apocalyptic art of the time and the proximity of the world to nuclear war in the early 1960s. 'The Castaway' presents a trapped Crusoe without self-belief, without any prospect of entering the Kingdom of Heaven through the needle's eye: '[t]he starved eye devours the seascape for the morsel/Of a sail/The horizon threads it infinitely'.[25] Alone and '[a]fraid lest my footprints multiply', he has only the company of 'dead metaphors' and metaphors of death – 'the green wine bottle's gospel choked with sand', and '[c]lenched sea-wood nailed and white as a man's hand' – this last is an image which combines crucifixion and clenched resistance, figuring the clenched pain of a slave victim thrown overboard. The violence and vileness of colonial history

33

are caught in that metonym, which exemplifies Walcott's determination '[t]o see things as they are, halved by a darkness/From which they cannot shift'.[26]

One area of 'darkness' that particularly seems to present difficulties in my reading of Derek Walcott's writing, however, is in his monologic representation of women, who tend to be Mothers, Muses or Madonnas. Too often his work reflects the patriarchal attitudes within colonial and indigenous cultures in which he grew up.[27] Many of Walcott's poems appear to recycle archetypal, male-constructed images of women, and indeed not only fail to give women a voice, but at times to recognise them as human. In *Another Life*, for example, the narrator recalls his adolescent lust for the painted 'shepherdesses of Boucher and Fragonard/and I raved for/the split pear of their arses/their milk-jug bubs'.[28]

All too often Walcott's 'adult' poetry displays similarly reductive attitudes to women, fixing them, whilst feeding off them. In the satirical poem, 'New World', for example, Eve is excluded altogether. Not surprisingly, given its title, 'A Lesson for This Sunday' focuses upon Sin, and is also set in a Caribbean paradise.[29] The narrator idly swinging in his hammock becomes aware of two children experimenting scientifically with yellow-wing butterflies. Cruelty is not just a feature of colonist-colonised relations, the text recognises, but a fact of the human condition: '[h]eredity of cruelty everywhere'. In the poem, however, it is the girl-child's cruelty that is singled out, as if it were somehow greater. 'The girl, in lemon frock', 'herself a thing of summery light/Frail as a flower in this blue August air' is fixed both as predator (compared to a mantis) and victim of Time ('and everywhere the frocks of summer torn'), as evanescent as the butterfly she destroys.

Patriarchal attitudes are not just dealt out to the young. In 'A Letter from Brooklyn', an old friend of his dead father writes a kindly letter about him, and though she is given a voice in writing, each of her lines is subjected to a somewhat patronising commentary:

'I am Mable Rawlins', she writes, 'and know both your parents';
He is dead, Miss Rawlins, but God bless your tense;
'Your father was a dutiful, honest,
Faithful, and useful person.'
For such plain praise what fame is recompense.[30]

Mable is reduced to a 'veined hand', and a face he cannot remember; her 'spidery style' inscribes a text he has difficulty reading. She becomes translated in the second half of the poem into a Muse figure, an ageing humble Penelope, one 'who spins the blessings of her years/Not withered of beauty if she can bring such tears'. Her act full of grace results in a return to faith 'and again I believe/I believe it all, and for no man's death I grieve.'

'Nights in the Gardens of Port of Spain' begins with a heavily 'feminised' Night, 'burning to be the bitch she will become', associated with 'secret and sweat' and an 'impenetrable musk'.[31] Although, clearly, the 'impenetrable' has sexual connotations, at the same time it gives a clue to Walcott's difficulties in his representation and understanding of women, as texts which cannot be read. 'Coral', which is even more melancholily erotic, again employs a feminised symbol of substance and absence, and ends: '[i]t dares my hand/To claim what lovers' hands have never known/The nature of the body of another.'[32]

Perhaps one of the most disturbing example of 'macho attitudes' in Walcott's writing is to be found in *Dream on Monkey Mountain*, whose climax sees Makak's attempted exorcism of the colonial presence figured in the beheading of the 'White Goddess'. The Corporal, suffering, like Makak, from 'that wrestling contradiction of being white in mind and black in body',[33] asserts that this white woman is:

> an image of your longing, as inaccessible as snow, as fatal as leprosy, Nun, virgin, Venus, you must violate, humiliate, destroy her ... She is all that is pure, all that he cannot reach. She is the colour of the law, religion, paper, art ... She is the white light that paralysed your mind, that led you into this confusion.[34]

Why white authority and oppression have to be incarnated in a woman, it is hard to say. Yet they are, for the male characters in *Dream on Monkey Mountain,* as they are for the aborigine Jimmie Blacksmith in Keneally's *The Chant of Jimmie Blacksmith*, whose fight back against the exploitation he has suffered begins with the killing of white women who have haunted his dreams and ambitions. Is Woman in both works seen as, in a sense, a legitimate target for violence since part of the colonised man's divided consciousness is still subject to the White Man? Are Makak and Jimmie attempting to right, and re-write themselves, sever themselves from vulnerability and submisssion by projecting their shame and self-hatred onto Woman, making Woman a fetish? Earlier in the play, however, Makak tells us it was this beautiful moon goddess/woman in white who had been the source of his articulation, whose singing had given birth to his voice:

> I see this woman singing
> And my feet grow roots. I could move no more.
> The snakes in my hair speak to one another,
> The smoke mouth open, and I behold this woman,

The loveliest thing I see on this earth,
Like the moon walking along her own road.[35]

Even later works such as 'The Schooner *Flight*' (1979), which I would regard as one of Walcott's finest lyric poems, continue with male stereotyping of women. These might seem 'appropriate' for its sailor-narrator. Shabine perhaps is redeemed to some extent by the severity of his suffering and his sense of guilt and remorse at his own treachery; he has abandoned wife and children for the love of Maria Concepcion, who in turn he leaves. She is both Muse and mate – the object of his lyric and painful desire – both a secular Mary, and star of his sea:

I knew when dark-haired evening put on
her bright silk at sunset, and, folding the sea,
sidled under the sheet with her starry laugh,
that there'd be no rest, there'd be no forgetting ...
I want those round brown eyes like a marmoset ...
those claws that tickled my back on sweating
Sunday afternoons, like a crab on wet sand.[36]

Maria never speaks, but she does throw plates. She is bridal, laced and silky, but also '*la belle dame sans merci*', whose beauty 'had fallen on me like a sword/cleaving me from my children, flesh of my flesh'. Although she seems like poetry, personified longing, rather she is a painful alternative to it, because she resists his wording. She is 'a harbour' that Shabine abandons, in favour of manipulable Poetry, 'the window I can look from that frames my life'. Perhaps Shabine senses that 'Homer's easier to live with'.

Walcott's contributions to literature and to enabling us to re-read literature have been considerable, but the attitudes to gender encoded within his poems to some extent detract from the scope and scale of his artistic and cultural achievement.

NOTES

1. David Dabydeen, *Turner: New and selected poems*, London 1994, xxi, 33.

2.   Sidney Burris, 'An Empire of Poetry', *The Southern Review*, 27:3 (1991), 558–74. Reprinted in Michael Parker and Roger Starkey, eds., *Post-Colonial Literatures: A new casebook*, Basingstoke 1995 (forthcoming).

3.   Derek Walcott, 'The Muse of History', quoted in David Dabydeen, ed., *A Handbook for Teaching Caribbean Literature*, Oxford 1988, 100.

4.   Derek Walcott, 'What the Twilight Says: An overture', in *Dream on Monkey Mountain and Other Plays*, London 1972, 17.

5.   Derek Walcott, *Omeros*, London 1990, 200.

6.   Derek Walcott, *Collected Poems 1948–1984*, New York 1986, 147.

7.   James Joyce, *Ulysses*, Harmondsworth 1986, 6.

8.   Walcott, *Collected Poems*, 200.

9.   ibid., 3.

10.   ibid.

11.   ibid., 11.

12.   ibid., 14.

13.   ibid., 360.

14.   ibid., 15–16.

15.   Susan Willis, 'Caliban as Poet: Reversing the maps of domination', *The Massachussetts Review*, Winter 1982, 615.

16.   Walcott, *Dream on Monkey Mountain*, part 1, scene 2, 286–7.

17.   ibid., 297.

18. Jean-Paul Sartre, 'Preface', to Frantz Fanon, *The Wretched of the Earth*, Harmondsworth 1967, 17. Walcott cites this passage in the epigraph to part 2 of *Dream on Monkey Mountain*.

19. ibid.

20. Walcott, *Collected Poems*, 17.

21. ibid., 356.

22. Edward Said, from *Orientalism*, quoted in Antony Easthope and Kate McGowan, eds., *A Critical and Cultural Theory Reader*, Buckingham 1992, 62.

23. John Carey, *The Intellectuals and the Masses*, London 1992, 208.

24. Gerald Moore, 'Reversing the Middle Passage', in M. T. Bindella and G. V. Davis, eds., *Imagination and the Creative Impulse in the New Literatures in English*, Amsterdam 1993, 87.

25. Walcott, *Collected Poems*, 57.

26. ibid., 66.

27. See also Elaine Savory Fido, 'Macho Attitudes and Derek Walcott', in Dennis Walder, ed., *Literature in the Modern World*, Oxford 1991, 288–94.

28. Walcott, *Collected Poems*, 202.

29. ibid., 39.

30. ibid., 41.

31. ibid., 67.

32. ibid., 73.

33. Walcott, 'What the Twilight Says: An overture', 12.

34.   ibid., 318–19.

35.   ibid., 227.

36.   Walcott, *Collected Poems*, 346–7.

5

'This coon condition': David Dabydeen's *The Intended*

David Ellis

I have chosen David Dabydeen as the subject of this essay because he at once maintains what might be described as a tradition within a tradition in Caribbean writing, and also because he brings to bear some of the characteristics of that tradition to a specific moment in British cultural and social history.

The tradition I speak of is that of the Indo-Caribbean writer. There can be little dispute that the terms of indentured Indian labour were different to those endured under the African slave trade, and one result of this has been that the theme of identity which has been traditionally associated with writing from the Caribbean, is dealt with rather differently by the Indo-Caribbean writers. Certainly, there seems to be a greater propensity among these writers to inhabit multiple identities in their writing, drawn on the cosmopolitan nature of the Caribbean. The late Sam Selvon is a clear example with his mix of characters in both the Trinidad and London novels, and this equates with his own concepts of creolisation and the Caribbean Man. Similarly, Wilson Harris revels in an absence of boundaries which extends beyond mere questions of personal identity.

Dabydeen maintains these concerns, and translates them into the debate surrounding the use of the term 'Black British', not just as it might be applied to writing, but to wider questions of national identity. He was born in 1955 into a family which, like Selvon's, had not maintained strict adherence to Hindu or Moslem traditions. Unlike Selvon, however, he was not brought up in a cosmopolitan atmosphere thriving on a mixture of races. Instead, his early childhood was disrupted by the violence between the Indians and blacks which marked and marred the negotiations for Guyanese independence. Living in the predominantly Afro-Caribbean New Amsterdam at the time, his family were regularly obliged to move back to the Indian villages in rural Berbice to escape the rioting.

This experience, he says, intensified 'one's nascent sense of Indianness',[1] not in terms of a revived religious commitment, but in a deep identification with the land. Guyana has the largest Indo-Caribbean population in the Caribbean, and this occupied many of the rural villages deserted by emancipated blacks who had opted for the cities. Dabydeen's Indianness, then, was one focused on mud huts and paddy-fields, rather than the cinematic images of India as a glorious place, 'full of wealth and opulence, of people and palaces'.[2] This sense of being an

Indo-Caribbean, rather than an Asian, was complicated by Dabydeen's emigration to Britain to join his father in 1969. His experience there, during the popular fascism of Powellism and skinhead violence, incurred the same feeling of displacement and threat as his Guyanese childhood, but with a tangible difference. During his childhood in Britain, Dabydeen, as a Caribbean immigrant, regarded Ugandan and Kenyan Asians as comparative 'outsiders' to British society, suffering the 'disadvantages of an alien language, alien foods and ways of dressing'.[3] At the same time, though, he can recount the sense of shame – fictionalised in *The Intended* – of being associated with those Asians:

> I think ... we became as integrated, in a negative sense, as possible, when we grew up. We would put little earrings in our ears, or smoke a bit of dope, or we would go dancing and argue the merits of David Bowie's music against that of T. Rex ... And what is sad is that it meant that as soon as you had the freedom to leave your parents, you dropped as quickly as possible that which was Asian about yourself.[4]

The negative aspect of this process of assimilation has since become central to Dabydeen's work. His progress as an academic critic and lecturer, as well as a poet and novelist, has centred around the project of bringing Britain's marginalised cultures to the centre; a reply, in many ways, to the Powellite rhetoric of his childhood that asserted an inviolate white nationhood. This project is best exemplified in Dabydeen's early work on Hogarth's *Blacks*, and more recently in his long poem on Turner's *Slave Ship*.

Dabydeen compares this quest to identify a black presence in the privileged arena of English fine art, with his own progress into Cambridge and Oxford:

> [i]t was an attempt to show that English art has a dimension of blackness to it; in other words, and on a personal level, that I belonged to British society ... You had to take what was defined as English high culture and find yourself in there.[5]

This work was intended to demonstrate that the black presence was not subordinate to the master culture, but a contributory aspect of it. Dabydeen thus celebrates a 'multiple identity'.[6] He extends Selvon's notion of creolisation and the Caribbean man through the Anancy myth, with the image of a spider figure having a series of poetic feet planted in the Guyanese, South American, Indian, African and European cultures. Instead of striving for a stable community, he says, you should 'adventure into the realms of anarchy and confusion which is the modern condition'.[7] This does not represent a loss of cultural identity, but rather the opportunity to exploit the potential energy in its multiplicity.

In Dabydeen's fiction, this notion is enacted both through individual characters and the society in which they operate. In both *The Intended* and his second novel, *Disappearance*, the central characters are confronted by their unquestioning acceptance of a western, empirical education. In the course of the narrative, this certainty becomes tempered by what Wilson Harris would term 'curative doubt', and with that doubt they learn to see through a colonial view of the Mother Country.

As one may gather from the title, *The Intended* uses Conrad's *Heart of Darkness* as a reference point. This occurs on several levels. The narrator, a young Guyanese immigrant left in care by his father, attempts to improve his lot through success in his 'A' Levels and entry to university. One might thus see in this text as parallel journey to Marlow's. The narrator's migration up the Thames from the Asian districts of South London to the university at Oxford, implies a similar stripping of personal authenticity in search of the polite savagery of the Oxbridge voice.

This, however, is not a simple novel about emigrant identity, but about the polyglot identity of enmeshed cultures. Dabydeen, in exploring the narrator's determination to assimilate himself into the colonial centre simultaneously illuminates the residual myths of colonialism and argues his own case for bringing marginalised cultures to the centre of the British identity. The narrator's progress through the English literature syllabus at once feeds his own aspirant status and provides Dabydeen with the opportunity to reinvest the images of literary analysis with their modern social significance.

The narrator's prowess at English Literature is based upon his ability to apply the theme of appearance and reality. This well-schooled technique leads him to interpret Conrad's text with ease:

> animal images, as a rule betokened moral ugliness, indecency and the like ... Reference to birds and fish on the other hand tended to betoken gentleness, spirituality, freedom. By counting the number of animal images against those of of fish or bird, it was easy to pinpoint that the work tended towards horror, or relief from horror. Since there were only two fish/bird allusions in the text as opposed to two dozen clear animal ones, it was obvious how Conrad felt about life in the Congo.[8]

The narrator's facility for reading his own existence through the terms of such literary imagery is made clear by his attempts to base his seduction of his girlfriend on the terms of *Troilus and Criseyde* (121). Janet, having come from a Kentish background and unsullied by the multi-cultural metropolis, is viewed as an English rose to be protected and revered in the traditions of chivalry (244). The narrator's own self-image, his 'coon condition' (230), is maintained by *Heart of Darkness* and the thematic associations described above.

The narrator's uncritical acceptance of these associations is an echo of Lamming's notion whereby Caliban learns language as an instrument of the exploring consciousness; the narrator learns the language, and thereby limits his consciousness. Dabydeen emphasises this process through the character of Joseph Countryman, a totally uneducated, young black Rasta whom the narrator meets at the Boy's Home.

Joseph's intuitive understanding of the operation of language as a system of social signifiers allows him to expose this system as a limit to the consciousness. The literary rules with which the narrator learns to understand poetry become a means by which '[y]ou turning all the room in the universe and in the human mind into bird cage' (95). Moreover, Joseph understands the extension of this signifying practice into social perceptions: '[w]hen I was in borstal I was rumour. They look at me and they see ape, trouble, fist ... all the time they seeing you as animal, riot, nigger, but you know you is nothing, atoms, only image and legend in their minds' (101).

Joseph brings the theme of appearance and reality to a dramatic conclusion in the text. His original intention to film a revised *Heart of Darkness* on his stolen video camera, becomes supplanted by a fascination with the space between things; with 'nothingness, colourlessness, the sightlessness of air, wind, the pure space between trees' (133). Joseph is trying to escape (or grasp) the invisible system of associations by which he has been locked into his own coon condition. Ultimately, he sees himself locked in by a word:

[i]t's me, all of that is me ... here is C and this one here is O and another C and two more O's, and then N ... Look! C is half O ... it nearly there, but it form O it breaking up again, never completing ... A is for apple ... B is for bat, C is for cocoon, which is also coon, N is for nut, but it's really for nuts, N is for nothing, N is for nignog. Can't you see, all of it is me (194–5).

Joseph escapes his condition through self-immolation. Through this act he transforms himself; the appearance of black flesh becomes reduced to a human reality of white ashes.

Joseph's visionary aspect casts him as a perennial alien in Britain. His institutionalised past prepares him only for imprisonment in the future, and he is street-wise enough to know that criminalisation is the lot of alternative voices and counter-cultures in Britain: '[i]f you talk peace, they think you only smoking weed. Is a dangerous thing to preach feelings and oneness. They prefer you to hang around cars' (87). By comparison, the narrator's two friends from school, Shaz and Patel, embrace the ideological morality of the Thatcherite market economy with zeal. Shaz becomes a pimp, and collaborates with Patel, who uses his father's corner shop business to finance and front drug-dealing and an amateur pornographic video industry. As Patel puts it: '[a]ll they [the whites] have over us is money ... and any monkey can make money, once you learn the trick' (245).

Benita Parry argues that the two boys' consequent facility in 'the inert jargon of Business Plans or the brutalised vocabulary of sex magazines' condemns them to the margins of British society.[9] One might argue, however, that such discourse is no more marginal than the language of literary analysis that the narrator goes to learn in the 'guarded walls of the library where entry is strictly forbidden to all but a select few' (195). In fact, both boys, by participating enthusiastically in the culture of supply and profit, are participating thereby in the master culture. Moreover, they recognise that in doing so, they are forfeiting their ancestral culture. As Patel says, 'Oxford has only got money, but the Asian community made you rich' (231).

The narrator's memories of Guyana are clouded by his determination to shed his colonial condition, and thus he is unable to identify these riches. His recollections, however, whilst they convey an impoverished and violent society, both in urban New Amsterdam and rural Albion Village, represent a counter-cultural voice akin to Joseph's in the text. The spontaneous generation of popular myths, a language rich in metaphor and a strong undercurrent of communal superstition all combine to illustrate a society free of a gridlock mentality. Thus, his Auntie Clarice's parting comment, 'you is we, remember you is we' (40), haunts the narrator in his efforts to join a British society based on division and delineation.

The narrator's quest for assimilation is, perhaps bizarrely, a recognition of these divisions. He does not want to become 'a lump of aborted, anonymous flesh' (198), but rather take on the finely chiselled features of Academia; his appearance will be outweighed by an academic reality that commands respect. His immature dream that when Janet returns from three years studying in Australia, he 'will have become something definite, my education compensating for my colour in the eyes of her parents' (245), is somehow vindicated by the position from which he writes his retrospective account: 'I am no longer an immigrant here, for I can decipher the texts' (195). In the process, though, he has developed a 'dark shadow ... [a] dark self' (196), which, like the society he has embodied, will not go away.

NOTES

1. Frank Birbalsingh, 'Interview with David Dabydeen', *Kunapipi*, 22:3 (1990), 104.

2. ibid., 105.

3. ibid., 117.

4. Wolfgang Binder, 'Interview with David Dabydeen', *Journal of West Indian Literature*, 3:2 (1989), 70.

5. ibid., 71–2.

6. Birbalsingh, op. cit., 118.

7. ibid., 119.

8. David Dabydeen, *The Intended*, London 1992, 94–5. Further page references are given in the text.

9. Benita Parry, 'David Dabydeen's *The Intended*', *Kunapipi*, 23:3 (1991), 87.

6

Britannia Major: writing and unionist identity

Willy Maley

Anyone majoring in British history will be well aware of the complexities of unionism. It would be a mistake, of course, to think that there was only one kind of union, that union was a bad thing, or that unionism and nationalism are somehow incompatible. There have been many unions, with attendant conquests and plantations, in British history. English nationalism and one anglocentric form of unionism have co-existed quite comfortably. Non-English nationalisms are not fundamentally at odds with unionism as such. The republican and nationalist Fletcher of Saltoun, for example, was not flatly against any political accommodation with England, but he was adverse to the incorporating union of 1707 that abolished the Edinburgh parliament. Many other opponents of incorporating union were far from being advocates of 'independence within Europe'. Subjection to England and complete separation are two extremes.

The fact that the two instantly recognisable unionist parties are based in Northern Ireland is significant, but that the Six Counties are the focal point for one forceful manifestation of unionism should not blind us to the reality that the British state is by and large a Union-state – not a nation-state but a four-nation state – that a unionist party is in power, that the major Opposition parties are unionist, or that far from British nationalism being a fringe phenomenon of the extreme right, it is the ideology that informs almost every party in the British state other than Plaid Cymru, Sinn Fein, the SNP, and the SDLP. Unionism remains a major force, perhaps *the* major force, in British politics today.

I want to introduce two texts that offer a sidelight on the long and difficult history of British unionism. Some degree of confusion exists as to what constitutes *national* identity, as opposed to, say, unionist identity, given that identity is always multiple and fractured. The fact that the British government had to resort to an electoral pact with Ulster Unionists in 1993 to get agreement on the Maastricht Treaty points up the way in which the Tory Party – still known in Scotland by its full title of Conservative and Unionist Party – sees Britishness as a buttress against Europe and a means of sustaining its grip on the Nation, by which it means the multi-nation British state.

Hegel's famous remark that all tragic events in history repeat themselves as farce finds a proof of sorts in two historical figures by the name of John Major, both British unionists, separated by almost 500 years of history. In 1521, a

Scottish humanist intellectual based in France wrote in Latin a pro-unionist *History of Greater Britain (Historia Majoris Britanniae* [Paris, 1921], punningly known as *Major's Britain*), which argued that although there were two kingdoms on the island, all of its inhabitants were Britons. Its author, by a curious quirk of history, bears the same name as the present leader of the Conservative and Unionist Party, who, in 1992, set out his own justifications for the Union. I want to juxtapose two texts by two John Majors, one Scottish and one English, an early-sixteenth century pro-unionist history and a late twentieth-century pre-election speech published as a pamphlet.[1] Henceforth, to distinguish between my two John Majors, I shall refer to the proto-unionist professor as Major Major, and the present Prime Minister as Major Minor.

Major Major was a lowlander, a borderer, born around 1470 in Gleghornie, North Berwick, in Lothian, 'the most civilised part of Scotland'. He described himself as a 'Scottish Briton', but he was also a good European. Major Major, despite 'being of ignoble birth', studied at Christ's College in Cambridge and at the Colleges of Navarre, Montagu, and Sorbonne in Paris. In the sixteenth century, one was arguably more likely to meet a Scot, at least an educated Scot, in Paris than in London. At the same time, fewer Englishmen were studying abroad, because of the growth of Oxbridge and national consciousness. Oxbridge was not always a kind host to northerners. From 1436 Scottish students enrolled in the German Nation of Paris colleges, rather, than as previously, the English Nation. If Major Major represented Renaissance Man, Major Minor had a rather more humble schooling, and represents Classless Man.

Major Major's pupils in Paris included the famous Belgian Peter of Brussels, Pierre Crockaert, who went on to become an eminent professor at Sorbonne. Back in Scotland, Major Major taught at Glasgow, where he had John Knox as a pupil, and at St. Andrews, where one of his students was George Buchanan, later a colleague in Paris. Buchanan, a highlander by extraction, and tutor to the young James VI, was an implacable opponent of Union. He also wrote his history in Latin *De Jure Regni Apud Scotos* (Edinburgh, 1579), and *Rerum Scoticarum* (Edinburgh, 1582). Buchanan was no great admirer of his former teacher, and in turn, James VI of Scotland, tutored by Buchanan, was not fond of him. James became the first historical King of Britain, flying in the face of Buchanan's promotion of the principle of Scottish sovereignty.

Major Major was thinking big when he chose to write his history of greater Britain in Latin. He was also thinking like a good European. It was not a question of choosing between Britain and Europe, or between expansionist England and the Auld Alliance with France, but of an equal union of two nations on one island in the interests of peace and security. Major Major was noted for his 'Sorbonnic style'. Sorbonne Latin was a modish version of a medium that was gradually going out of fashion as the universal language of learning. Had he elected to write in the vernacular, his text would have been better known. There were only two editions – Paris (1521) and Edinburgh (1740) – before the English translation published by the Scottish History Society in 1892 as *The History of Greater Britain*. By the nineteenth century, of course, Greater Britain had come to refer to the colonies of the British Empire.

A century later, Major Minor's treatise on the British union was published as Europe became a single market. Major Minor called his text *Scotland in the United Kingdom*. It was first delivered in Glasgow on 22nd February 1992 as a speech to a conference of prospective parliamentary and district council candidates, and printed the following month. Major Minor fought the General Election of that year on an unyielding unionist platform in Scotland, equating devolution with independence as a threat to the Union. On this occasion, he first reminds his audience that, although they are now in a minority, the Tories held the majority of seats in Scotland in the 1950s under the banner of unionism. Under the sub-heading of 'The Wider World', he tells them that in Scotland they will meet 'people with pride in the role this United Kingdom – Scotland and Wales, England and Northern Ireland *together* – has played in world affairs – in helping to liberate Kuwait, to safeguard the Kurds, to promote the U.N., to help build democracy in the old Soviet Union and to put Europe on the right path.' Major Minor asserts that 'Britain is now exerting unique influence on world affairs. And when I say that I am not thinking only of the Gulf War in which Scottish service men and women played such an heroic part. I am thinking of the everyday currency of peace-time diplomacy.' Of course, Thatcher had the Falklands and Major Minor had the so-called Gulf War, brilliant opportunities to wrap themselves in the Union Jack. According to one estimate, 40% of British troops in the Gulf were Scots. Referring to 'The Perils of Scottish Independence', Major Minor warns against breaking 'the links through which we have worked together for nearly three hundred years', an allusion to the Union of Parliaments of 1707.[2] To look back further to the Anglo-Scottish Union of Crowns of 1603 would be to appeal to a unionism that goes beyond parliamentary sovereignty.

Putting his cards on the table, Major Minor says that he has come to:

> speak of a matter that transcends the election. To say again what I believe. I believe with passion and conviction that this Party should stand for unity – not division. We are a Unionist Party. We should fight for the Union.

He follows up by saying that although he does not defend the Union 'for party political advantage ... yet it is our Party that supports the Union. Not because it

has always been good for us, but because it has always seemed *right* to us.'
Major Minor moves on to 'shared values': 'only last week, in my flat in
London, I used television – a Scotsman's invention – to watch pictures of an
English game – cricket – being played in a city 12,000 miles away – Dunedin,
called after Scotland's capital.' Major Minor involves 'the defence of Britain,
for which so many Scotsmen have fought shoulder to shoulder with Englishmen,
Welshmen, and Ulstermen too.' Northern Ireland and 'Ulster' are not, of course,
coterminous. Only six of Ulster's nine counties are contained within the present
jurisdiction of the British state. Major Minor speaks of 300 years of Anglo-
Scottish history but confines himself to 70 years of Anglo-Irish history, since the
Partition of Ireland. Here, any reference to the failed Union of Great Britain and
Ireland of 1800 would undermine Major Minor's argument, which relies on a
single unionist vision.

Within that single vision, Major Minor promotes a notion of dual identity:
'to each of us, the Union has offered two sources of pride. To be British – but
also to be Scottish, or English or Welsh. It has offered the same assurance to the
people of Northern Ireland.' Has it? What are the two sources of pride in
Northern Ireland? To be Irish and Catholic or British and Protestant? He points
out: '[i]n sport, we can compete with each other – and still come together as
Britons.' Remember the ill-fated 'Home Internationals', which threatened to
trigger an Anglo-Scottish war? Major Minor puts his finger on the crux of the
matter: 'if the Union of our four countries [Ireland now included as a whole]
had never been founded our history would have been entirely different, our
destiny far less great.' Major Minor spells out the consequences of Scottish
separatism: 'a solitary Scotland means a solitary England, alongside Wales and
Northern Ireland. Two proud nations, divorced, marginalised, diminished. In
place of Great Britain, a little Scotland and a lesser Union – each striving, and
not always succeeding, to be heard.' Major Minor concludes by observing that:
'it is not fanciful to say that together the peoples of these islands have moulded
the history of the world. Separating or separated we would be tossed to and fro
on its tides', and his closing vision is of: 'a confident and united Scotland in a
confident and united Britain.'

Major Major called his history *Britannia Major*, partly to play on his own
name, partly to distinguish between Britain and Brittany – known as 'Britannia
Minor' – and partly, of course, as a call for the two kingdoms to aggrandise
themselves and resolve into one. It is perhaps worth noting that until the
eleventh century Ireland was known in medieval Latin as 'Scotia Major' and
Scotland as 'Scotia Minor'. In his dedicatory preface to James V, whom he
praises for his 'lofty descent in the line of both kingdoms of Greater Britain',
Major Major introduces himself as 'John, Major by name, Scot by nation,

theologian of the university of Paris by profession'. He distinguishes between southern Scots, or 'household Scots', like himself, and the 'Wild Scots' of the highlands and islands. One key feature of Major Major's history is his rejection of the British origin myths being marketed by English historians. He is particularly keen to scotch the brute that the Scots, like the Welsh, are descended from Brutus. Indeed, although he styles himself a 'Scottish Briton' he insists that 'the Irish are descended from the Spaniards and the Scottish Britons from the Irish.' Where Edmund Spenser will claim that the Irish are really Scots, Major contends that the Scots are really Irish. Major Major also draws a line between Britain and Ireland. He mentions in passing that King Gregory of Scotland conquered Ireland in 875 but does not seem too troubled by its subsequent loss.

George Buchanan would later uphold the Scottish interest in Ireland against the competing claim of England. In the wake of the Union of Crowns, the Ulster Plantation allowed Anglo-Scottish differences over Ireland to be resolved and led ultimately to an English Pale around Dublin being, in an act of upward displacement, superseded by a British Pale around Belfast. Major Minor makes no mention in the Downing Street Declaration of the constitutional status of Northern Ireland having some relation to that of Scotland, with its future ultimately dependent on a referendum.

Major Major also argues for a dual identity. He wants to adopt the term British as a political and geographical rather than an ethnic or national identity. He rails against English appropriations of Britishness. In 1522, the year after *Britannia Major* was published, the editor of Ptolemy's *Geography* applied the phrase to England alone: 'Britannia Major cui nomen est Anglia'. This is an early instance of England seeing itself as Britain, something that has been all too common since. Major Major wants to pre-empt an incorporating union, and the overweening Englishing of Britain. He is 'not wont to credit the common Scot in his vituperation of the English, nor yet the Englishman in his vituperation of the Scot.' He states that 'two neighbouring kingdoms striving for the mastery, never cherish a sincere desire for peace.' He points out that 'though the English became masters of Aquitane, Anjou, Normandy, Ireland and Wales, they have up to this date made no way in Scotland.' He insists that:

[t]he Scots ought to prefer no king to the English in the marriage of the female heir, and I am of the same opinion as to the English in a similar case. By this way only two hostile kingdoms flourishing in the same island, of which neither can subdue the other, would be united under one king, and it is said the Scots would lose their name and kingdom, so would the English, for the king of both would be called king of Britain.[3]

Major Major wants peace through royal intermarriage and a union of crowns. He reminds Scots readers of the English provenance of James V (Margaret Tudor, the daughter of Henry VII, having married James IV of Scotland), and goes on to declare that: 'the Scots kings should marry with the daughters of the English kings, and contrariwise; and thus, some day, shall one of them come to have a lawful right to all Britain; for without such a lawful right I see not how the Scots shall master the English, nor yet the English the Scots.' Francis Bacon, in his *History of King Henry VII*, records that some of Henry's counsellors cautioned:

> that if God should take the King's two sons without issue, that then the kingdom of England would fall to the King of Scotland, which might prejudice the monarchy of England. Whereunto the King replied; That if that should be, Scotland would be but an accession to England, and not England to Scotland; for the greater would draw the less; and it was a safer union for England than that of France.[4]

'Union' with France, of the 'Auld Alliance', was consolidated in 1558 with the marriage of Francis and Mary, from whence Scots were naturalised in France. This was confirmed by Henry IV in 1599. Englishmen could purchase the same rights but only at the expense of becoming aliens in England. Major Major says that there were once nine or ten kingdoms in Britain, and that the Scots now hold the kingdom of the Picts while the English hold the kingdom of the Welsh. He argues that Wales, conquered by England, is in a quite different position from that of Scotland. He anticipates that the nobility of both England and Scotland will oppose a union of crowns because they do not wish to have an all-powerful king over them, but that such an absolute monarch would actually benefit the aristocracy.

It is not surprising that one of the first calls for union should have come from a European Scot. At a time when England was turning its back on Europe and expanding its power base in Ireland, some Scottish intellectuals saw some form of union as inevitable and wanted one on their terms. Major Major did not like William Caxton, whom he held to have not only printed *The Chronicles of England*, known as *Caxton's Chronicles*, a reproduction of the *Chronicle of Brut*, but to have written it as well. Here was a history of Britain for English nationalists rather than British unionists.

Major Major's unionism is very different from that of Major Minor. It is also quite distinct from the positions taken up by post-reformation Scottish historians in the sixteenth century. David Chambers, a lord of the Court of Session, wrote a Catholic history in French, published in Paris in 1579, which celebrated the

Scottish alliance with France. James Harrysone, an Edinburgh merchant, wrote one in English that was Protestant, apocalyptic, and imperialist, the *Godly and Golden Book for Concorde of England and Scotland* (1547). George Buchanan wrote (in Latin) as part of the so-called 'retreat from Britain' that coincided with the English 'retreat from Europe' and expansion within an enlarged Britain, conceived of as including the separate island of Ireland. The languages in which these histories were written – French, Latin, and English – say something about the perspective of the various authors. Much could be said about the effects of anglocentric union. In 1500 half of the 'British Isles' was Celtic speaking. By 1650 the figure was less than one-tenth. It may be that the loss of European languages is linked to the loss of Welsh, Scots, and Irish tongues.

It is a long way from Berwick to Brixton, and from the Britain of Major Major to the Britain of Major Minor, from a minor Jacobean to a major Elizabethan, but unionism remains a major issue. European union, major union, sits awkwardly beside British union, minor union. Unionism at large, or unionism writ large. Keith Robbins has suggested that 'British history', one level, ended with the United Kingdom's entry into the European Community in 1975.[5] Reports of the death of Great Britain are greatly exaggerated. The British state persists in its anomalous and increasingly eccentric policy of 'independence within Europe'. British sovereignty is historically at odds with closer European unity. Indeed, 'Britain' was first and foremost an alternative to Europe, another continent, Europe Minor. The Atlanticism and anti-federalism of Major Minor are evident. If he had had the benefit of a university education, or had the history of his namesake been more widely available, he could have learned a lot from Major Major.

Between Major Major and Major Minor there lies the fraught matter of Britain from a Scottish perspective, of unionism both major and minor, of Great Britain, and of Greater Britain. If it was a Scot who coined the phrase *Britannia Major*, and who first outlined a vision of Major's Britain, then it is worth recalling that it was also a Scot, James Thomson, who in 1740 composed one of the best-known cultural celebrations of British imperialism – *Rule Britannia*.

NOTES

1.   John Major, ed. and trans. Archibald Constable, *Historia Majoris Britanniae tam Angliae quam Scotiae*, Paris 1921, *John Major's History of Greater Britain*, Scottish History Society (1st series, no. 10) Edinburgh 1892; John Major, *Scotland in the United Kingdom*, London 1992.

2. *Scotland in the United Kingdom*, op. cit., 7.

3. *John Major's History of Greater Britain*, op. cit., lxxix.

4. James Spedding, Robert Leslie Ellis, and Douglas Denon Heath, eds., *The Works of Francis Bacon* (15 vols.), London 1857–74, Vol. VI, 216.

5. Keith G. Robbins, *Insular Outsider? 'British History' and European Integration: The Stenton lectures 1989*, Reading 1990, 15.

7

'As a woman I have no country':
Woolf and the construction of national identity

Clare Hanson

My title quotation comes from Woolf's polemical pacifist text *Three Guineas*, which was published in 1938 and responds very directly to its contemporary context, the Spanish Civil War and the threat of the Second World War. The full quotation runs: '[f]or, the outsider will say, in fact, as a woman, I have no country. As I woman I want no country. As a woman my country is the whole world.'[1]

Woolf makes an unambiguous claim here for the difference of view of the outsider and/or the woman in relation to national identity. Because the woman is not interpellated as a subject within the plural 'we' of national identity, she, in turn, will not recognise such identity. She will discover within herself, writes Woolf, no 'patriotic emotion', for if she questions herself she will find that 'our country ... throughout the greater part of its history has treated me as a slave.'[2] Woolf's position, articulated in 1938, bears similarities with that of Homi Bhabha and Julia Kristeva, who have each argued recently that a marginal (or 'outsider') position makes for a radically different understanding of national and cultural identity. I want to use their work as a starting point for considering Woolf's attitude to national or English identity.

Homi Bhabha, in his recent book *The Location of Culture*, has argued that postcolonial experience offers a new perspective from which to understand the means by which the social imaginary (nation, culture or community) becomes 'the subject of discourse and the object of psychic identification'.[3] He insists that nationness is a matter of social and textual affiliation (i.e., that nation is constructed through narration), and argues that traditional nationalist narratives are couched in terms of teleology, while, paradoxically, taking place in what he calls 'a horizontal, homogeneous empty time'. Drawing on the work of Fanon and Foucault, as well as on Derrida, Bhabha suggests that the marginalised, postcolonial outsider can, however, insinuate him/herself into this dominant narrative. Once there, the outsider, figured by Bhabha as 'the supplementary':

> antagonizes the implicit power to generalise, to produce the sociological solidity. The questioning of the supplement is not a repetitive rhetoric of the 'end' of society but a meditation on the disposition of space and time from which the narrative of the nation must begin.[4]

It is not, then, that the dominant discourse is challenged by the 'outsider' in an antagonistic fashion: it is rather that the articulation of supplementarity can expose the metaphysical rather than the essential nature of the divisions on which national identity is founded. Such an articulation also calls into question the (imaginary) disposition of space and time which supports the discursive construction of national identity. In this connection, Bhabha offers a passionate critique of 'historical time', which he aligns with '[t]he dead hand of history that tells the beads of sequential time like a rosary, seeking to establish serial, causal connections.'[5] Not against but alongside this, he offers the possibility of a space which cuts across time, producing complex figures of difference and identity, past and present, inside and outside, inclusion and exclusion. This space is also figured as the 'beyond', an imagined space which Bhabha describes as 'beyond the border of our times'. It is as though space must be bent back into time, the multiple, discontinuous, unequal space of individual and nation.

Bhabha draws heavily here on the work of Julia Kristeva, who has theorised the relation between the individual and the nation not only in the recent *Strangers to Ourselves* (1991) but also in the earlier essay, 'Women's Time' (first published in 1979). In 'Women's Time', Kristeva too links the construction of the nation with 'a certain conception of time': 'time a project, teleology, linear and prospective unfolding: time as departure, progression and arrival – in other words, the time of history.'[6] Adopting, like Bhabha, the position of the outsider, Kristeva suggests that the perspective of *woman's* difference might point the way to a necessary reformulation of the concepts of time and nation. The 'third stage' of feminism which she imagines and invokes in this essay is thus figured as a space which cuts across the linear time of history, a 'corporeal and desiring mental space' in which conventional time, history and identity are all destabilised.[7] For Kristeva, the posing of the question of the other thus brings about a kind of arrest of the 'false time' of history and a suspension of habitual forms of identity and identification. And although Kristeva's work has been criticised for its supposed emphasis on personal identity, it must be stressed that for her the problematic of identity is always both personal and social, for in her view individual identity and social structure are indissolubly linked through the workings of the symbolic order. Her work has thus offered an invaluable resource for critics like Bhabha who are turning to the connection between individual and social identity in their attempt to found a new cultural hermeneutics. In 'Women's Time', Kristeva anticipates many recent discussions of the way in which cultural difference is constructed through processes of alterity. Her call in this essay for an 'interiorisation of the founding separation of the socio-symbolic contract' (to which I will return) also accords well with Bhabha's optimistic claim that: '[i]t is by living on the borderline of history and language, on the limits of race and gender, that we are in a position to translate the differences between them into a kind of solidarity.'[8]

Virginia Woolf's attitude to national identity has been very little commented on, surprisingly, in view of her exploration in *Three Guineas* of the connections between patriarchy, militarism and imperialism. Indeed, if we look back over Woolf's work, it is clear that one of her major preoccupations was the ambivalent nature of her connection with an English national (writing) identity. Repeatedly, in her fiction and in her essays, Woolf tells the story of English literature – but tells it with a difference. The history of English literature offers both presence and a past to the male writer as inheritor. It gives him a social identity, and seems to hold out the promise that he too will function as a representative, that is, dominant cultural figure like the writers of the past. For the woman, as Woolf repeatedly points out, there is no such position. Is this why, in *Orlando*, when Woolf comes to construct the history of a nation through its literature, she keeps interrupting and confounding the progress of linear time? When Orlando reaches the eighteenth century, for example, a kindly Captain points out Mr Addison, Mr Dryden and Mr Pope talking together in a coffee house, a chronological error which can, as Woolf's own footnote points out be corrected by a reference 'to any textbook of literature': still, the error is left to stand. This movement towards confusion is of course replicated in the wider structure of the book, in which Orlando's single life is made to hold all the periods of English literature together in what Gertrude Stein might call a continuous present. The multiplicity of 'individual' identity is comically stressed by Woolf in this text:

> For if there are (at a venture) seventy-six different times all ticking in the mind at once, how many different people are there not – Heaven help us – all having lodgement at one time or another in the human spirit? Some say two thousand and fifty-two.[9]

But more importantly, the multiplicity of social identity is also stressed. The 'periods' of English literature and of English history are brought together in a textual space in which different social values and identities compete and clash with each other. This discontinuous space, I would suggest, offers a metaphor also for the multiple and discordant nature of the 'present' moment. It is this multiplicity which the linear time of nation and history seeks to deny, in the interests of creating the narrative of the dominant group. Linear time insists on singularity, eliding the conflicting voices and identities of the marginalised or oppressed. As Bhabha writes: '[t]he political unity of the nation consists in a continual displacement of the anxiety of its irredeemably plural modern space.'[10]

In *A Room of One's Own* (written just after *Orlando*), Woolf similarly tells the story of English literature, this time still more clearly from the perspective of the dispossessed. And in gendering the history of English literature, Woolf again unsettles what Bhabha calls 'the disposition of space and time'. For just as *Orlando* is held together by the figure of Orlando her/himself, so *A Room of One's Own* is held together by the figure of Judith Shakespeare, the imagined sister of William. Judith Shakespeare has never lived, but is presented in the text both as having died and as capable of being reborn. Again the book, a space of conflict and disruption cuts across the linear time of history and nation.

Implicit in my argument in this essay is the belief that there was for Woolf, as for Kristeva, an indissoluble connection between individual identity and social identity. This is not, I would suggest, just a matter of a handy metaphor or rhetorically useful analogy. The connection can be understood in terms of Woolf's profound awareness of the sacrificial nature of the social contract. This is, of course, something which Kristeva has written about at length. For Kristeva, as Jacqueline Rose has written, '[t]he socio-symbolic contract is founded on a moment of violence, the violence of primitive psychic separation which precipitates subjects into language and the violence of a social order which has sacrifice as its symbolic base.'[11]

Kristeva suggests that because the socio-symbolic order offers, so to speak, different terms for men and for women, women 'experience this sacrificial contract against their will'.[12] Their response to this can take the form of an attempted refusal of the social bond, or it can take the form of a defensive over-investment in it. Alternatively – and this is where Kristeva sees grounds for hope – it can take the form of a self-analysis which explores the violence of the constitution of subjectivity *and* sociality.

In this connection, I want to look now at a passage in *The Waves* which has been overlooked by Woolf's critics. *The Waves* is generally regarded as Woolf's most inward and subjective novel, almost completely removed from social questions. However, in this novel, Woolf very clearly explores the link between the violence of subjectivity and the violence of the social order. The passage in question comes in the middle of the dinner held at Hampton Court to mark Percival's departure for India. Louis and Rhoda draw apart, and comment on the other characters. Louis is the first to speak:

They are savage; they are ruthless. They dance in a circle, flapping bladders. The flames leap over their painted faces, over the leopard skins and the bleeding limbs which they have torn from the living body.

The flames of the festival rise high, said Rhoda. The great procession passes, flinging green boughs and flowering branches. Their horns spill blue smoke; their skins are dappled red and yellow in the torchlight. They throw violets ... The procession passes. And while it passes, Louis, we are aware of downfalling, we forbode decay. The shadow slants. We who are conspirators, withdrawn together to learn over some cold urn, note how the purple flame flows downwards.[13]

In this passage Woolf links directly the violent egotism of the individual characters (their 'fell' attributes and purposes) and the violence which was, according to the anthropologists whom she was reading at the time, inherent in and constitutive of the social bond itself.[14] The social bond is created in part through the exclusion of 'others', and Woolf here explores the ways in which the social and national cohesion of the group at Hampton Court depends, ultimately, on the oppressions of Empire. In this respect, Percival acts out in exemplary fashion the kind of 'othering' of the Orient described by Said:

But now, behold, Percival advances; Percival rides a flea-bitten mare, and wears a sun helmet. By applying the standards of the West, by using the violent language that is natural to him, the bullock-cart is righted in less than five minutes. The Oriental problem is solved. [15]

But the cohesion of the group depends not only on the sacrifice of the 'multitudes' in the Orient, but also on the sacrifice of Percival himself, which is foreshadowed in the first passage quoted. It is his death which suggests so powerfully in this text the inherence of violence in the social order. Without violence there would be no order, and no social group.

By the time Woolf came to write *Three Guineas* (published seven years after *The Waves*), she had become still more preoccupied with questions of social identity and organisation. It is significant that at this time she was reading the later work of Freud, which is, of course, concerned with similar issues.[16] In *Three Guineas*, Woolf stresses again the indivisibility of public and private life, claiming that: '[t]he public and private worlds are inseparably connected ... the tyrannies and servilities of the one are the tyrannies and servilities of the other.'[17]

In this text, Woolf links patriarchy and patriotism, and argues that women simply do not share in the patriotic and nationalistic emotions which, at the time she was writing, were supporting the drift towards war. Woolf finds the idea of the nation completely antipathetic: women, she writes, are free of the 'stigma of nationality'.[18] The question arises whether women, in Woolf's view, lie in some sense outside the social contract? Certainly women do not conglomerate, and Woolf thinks that there may be something 'in the conglomeration of people into societies that releases what is most selfish and violent, least rational and humane in the individuals themselves.'[19]

In a passage drawing on the vocabulary of sacrifice and savagery also evident in *The Waves*, Woolf goes on to argue for the perniciousness of current forms of social organisation, and further underscores the arbitrary, non-essential nature of the divisions of race and nation which have been made by men. She writes:

> [i]nevitably we look upon societies as conspiracies that sink the private brother, whom many of us have reason to respect, and inflate in his stead a monstrous male, loud of voice, hard of fist, childishly intent upon scoring the floor the earth with chalk marks, within whose mystic boundaries human beings are penned, rigidly, separately, artificially; where, daubed red and gold, decorated like a savage with feathers he goes through mystic rites and enjoys the dubious pleasures of power and dominion.[20]

Woolf seems here to lay the blame unequivocally at *men's* door. Societies are constructed and maintained through a violence in which women do not share. But if Woolf is positioning women outside the social order, this would be the equivalent of the kind of refusal of the social bond which Kristeva sees as a negative response to women's experience of it. Kristeva identifies such a rejection of the symbolic with the 'second stage' of feminism and with a failure to grasp the true nature of women's relation to the social contract. She favours the more lucid approach which: 'without refusing or sidestepping this socio-symbolic order – consists in trying to explore the constitution and functioning of this contract, starting ... from the very personal affect experienced when facing it as subject and as a woman.'[21] This, in fact, is the path that Woolf takes: in other words, she moves beyond the negativity of rejection and attempts to analyse the symbolic in order to redefine it. Even in *Three Guineas*, which is Woolf's most scathing attack on patriarchal societies and on the social bond, there is a recognition of the inescapability of the social bond and an attempt to redefine it. This attempt at redefinition comes with Woolf's suggestion that those opposed to the war should form an 'Outsiders' Society'. Such a society represents a contradiction in terms of our current understanding of social order, but it can also be seen as an attempt to go beyond those terms and to think towards new forms of affiliation and identification – of modes of being at once inside and outside.

In *The Years*, published a year before *Three Guineas*, Woolf vividly dramatises these issues through the thoughts of North Pargiter, the most sympathetic character in the novel. North has been away farming in South

Africa, and returns to England to find himself, as he himself comments, 'an outsider'. At Delia's party, which represents society, North expresses views which seem to be very close to Woolf's own. He does not believe in 'joining societies, in signing manifestos', and is mistrustful both of organisations which seek to change the world, and of their rhetoric:

> What do they mean by Justice and Liberty? he asked, all these nice young men with two or three hundred a year. Something's wrong, he thought; there's a gap, a dislocation, between the word and the reality. If they want to reform the world, he thought, why not begin there, at the centre, with themselves?[22]

This idea of beginning 'at the centre, with themselves', is very close to Kristeva's notion of the 'interiorisation' of the symbolic, if we understand by such 'interiorisation' the recognition that the violence of subjectivity and of sociality and nationality can only be elided through the development of a new form of intersubjectivity. It is such a new intersubjective space which North seems to be evoking as he thinks of 'downing barriers' (personal and social) and floating on a stream of consciousness:

> [n]ot black shirts, green shirts, red shirts – always posing in the public eye; that's all poppycock. Why not down barriers and simplify? But a world, he thought, that was all one jelly, one mass, would be a rice pudding world, a white counterpane world. To keep the emblems and token of North Pargiter – the man Maggie laughs at; the Frenchman holding his hat; but at the same time spread out, make a new ripple in human consciousness, be the bubble and the stream, the stream and the bubble – myself and the world together – he raised his glass. Anonymously, he said.[23]

Woolf's image of the bubble and the stream points towards the kind of reformulation of the relation between self and world which has been called for from a postcolonial perspective by Bhabha and from a feminist perspective by Kristeva. The question which remains us is whether such a reformulation is simply a dream which must remain at the level of a 'revolution in poetic language' only. I would argue against this view. In his essay 'The Commitment to Theory', Homi Bhabha argues for the importance of 'theory' in shaping the world, in creating new possibilities to struggle for. He writes: '[w]hat is to be done? must acknowledge the force of writing, its metaphoricity and its rhetorical discourse, as a productive matrix which defines the 'social' and makes it available as an objective of and for, action.'[24] I would argue similarly for the importance of Woolf's poetic or metaphorical thinking about the self and the world, seeing it as part of a 'productive matrix' of modern thought which can and will change social and national formations.

Woolf's last novel, *Between the Acts*, written in the first months of the Second World War, offers a powerful challenge to those traditional beliefs about national identity which were, in Woolf's view, largely responsible for the contemporary crisis. In this novel Woolf turns again to the story of English history, a story which is here explicitly linked with the creation of national and imperial identity. Miss La Trobe's pageant, which renders this story, becomes an extravagant parody of hackneyed notions of 'English' identity from the Elizabethan period on. The audience expect this story to culminate in the traditional manner of an Empire Day Pageant, with a 'Grande Ensemble, round the Union Jack', but, of course, this expectation is not met.[25] Just as in *Orlando* and *A Room of One's Own*, Woolf subverts the linear narrative of national identity in this text, and the pageant ends not with a culminating scene, but in a-historical chaos, as characters from different periods appear together:

> behold Miss Whatshername behind the tree summoned from the bushes – or was it *they* who broke away – Queen Bess; Queen Anne; and the girl in the Mall; and the Age of Reason; and Budge the policeman; here they came. And the Pilgrims. And the lovers. And the grandfather's clock. And the old man with a beard. They all appeared. What's more, each declaimed some phrase or fragment from their parts ... *I am not* (said one) *in my perfect mind* ... Another, *Reason am I*.[26]

As in earlier texts, this multiplicity offers a metaphor for the plurality of 'the time of the nation': to return to Bhabha's phrase, the discordance reflects the 'anxiety of [the nation's] irredeemably plural modern space'. Woolf stops the narrative of national history and identity in its tracks, and shows instead the multiplicity of 'English' identity, its differences and discordances, particularly when seen from the point of view of a woman. When Miss La Trobe turns the mirrors on the audience, we see the plurality of 'our' identity, which is broken up, fragmented, disjointed. 'Ourselves' are 'in parts':

> Ourselves! Ourselves!
>
> Out they leapt, jerked, skipped. Flashing, dazzling, dancing, jumping. Now old Bart ... he was caught. Now Manresa. Here a nose ... There a skirt ... Then trousers only ... Now perhaps a face ... Ourselves? But that's cruel. To snap us as we are, before we've had time to assume ... And only, too, in parts ... That's what's so distorting and upsetting and utterly unfair.[27]

In this last part of *Between the Acts*, in which the text moves restlessly between the terms 'ourselves' and 'dispersed', Woolf stages one of her most radical insights, which is that if collective identity is multiple and plural, so too is individual identity, or rather, vice versa. One could summarise the argument, crudely, in the following terms. Woolf sees a continuity between the construction of individual, social and national identities, which are all founded on repression, exclusion and sacrifice. In the construction of individual identity, the unwelcome aspects of the self are repressed and stored in the unconscious; in the construction of social identity, 'scapegoats' take on the burden of representing what is rejected and deemed anti-social; in the construction of national identity, 'the foreigner' or 'the enemy' takes on the burden of representing all that which we would not wish to acknowledge as part of 'ourselves'. It is in recognising these processes, and in taking responsibility for the violence inherent in the construction of all identities, that we can move towards the possibility of re-visioning and re-making individual and social identities, of creating 'the bubble and the stream'. I would argue that Woolf certainly came to hold such a view through her exploration of the construction of individual, social and national identities in her later work. In *Between the Acts* this view or ethic is expressed in semi-comic form by the Rev. G. W. Streatfield, as he sums up the meaning of Miss La Trobe's pageant. He declares:

> [t]o me at least it was indicated that we are members one of another. Each is part of the whole. Yes, that occurred to me, sitting among you in the audience. Did I not perceive Mr Hardcastle here (he pointed) at one time a Viking? And in Lady Harridan – excuse me, if I get the names wrong – a Canterbury pilgrim? *We act different parts; but are the same.*[28]

We act different parts, but are the same: Woolf's insight here could not be more modern. There is in each of us the capacity to act many parts, but we can identify ourselves with only one: the same is true in the wider staging of social and national identities. However, in recognising, at least, the mechanisms of repression and projection which are involved in the construction of such identities, we take the first step towards deconstructing and reconstructing them. As Julia Kristeva writes in *Strangers to Ourselves*:

> [w]hen we flee from or struggle against the foreigner, we are fighting our unconscious that 'improper' facet of our impossible 'own and proper'. Delicately, analytically, Freud does not speak of foreigners: he teaches us how to detect foreignness in ourselves. That is perhaps the only way not to hound it outside of us. After Stoic cosmopolitanism, after religious

universalist integration, Freud brings us the courage to call ourselves disintegrated in order not to integrate foreigners and even less so to hunt them down, but rather to welcome them to that uncanny strangeness, which is as much theirs as it is ours.[29]

Or as Woolf put it in what could be called her political trilogy – the texts written under the shadow of the Second World War, *The Years*, *Three Guineas* and *Between the Acts* – we must begin here, at the centre, with our (dispersed) selves, if we are to hope to change the symbolic and political order.

NOTES

1.   Virginia Woolf, *A Room of One's Own*, Oxford 1992, 313.

2.   ibid., 313.

3.   Homi Bhabha, *The Location of Culture*, London 1994, 153.

4.   ibid., 155.

5.   ibid., 4.

6.   Julia Kristeva, 'Women's Time', in Toril Moi, ed., *The Kristeva Reader*, Oxford 1986, 192.

7.   ibid., 209.

8.   Bhabha, op. cit., 170.

9.   Virginia Woolf, *Orlando*, Oxford 1992, 294.

10.   Bhabha, op. cit., 149.

11.   Jacqueline Rose, *Why War?*, Oxford 1993, 43.

12.   Kristeva, op. cit., 200.

13.   Virginia Woolf, *The Waves*, Oxford 1992, 115.

14. For example, James Frazer, *The Golden Bough* (1922); Jane Harrison, *Prolegomena to the Study of Greek Religion* (1903).

15. Woolf, *The Waves*, 111.

16. In particular, Woolf was reading *Group Psychology and the Analysis of the Ego* in the 1930s, and *Moses and Monotheism* when she was drafting *Between the Acts*.

17. Virginia Woolf, *A Room of One's Own* and *Three Guineas*, Oxford 1992, 364.

18. ibid., 273.

19. ibid., 307–8.

20. ibid., 308.

21. Kristeva, op. cit., 200.

22. Virginia Woolf, *The Years*, Oxford 1992, 385.

23. ibid., 390.

24. Bhabha, op. cit., 23.

25. Virginia Woolf, *Between the Acts*, Oxford 1992, 141.

26. ibid., 166.

27. ibid., 165.

28. ibid., 172–3 (my italics).

29. Julia Kristeva, trans. L. S. Roudiez, *Strangers to Ourselves*, Hemel Hempstead 1991, 191–2.

8

'Between their titles and low name': Shakespeare, nation and the contemporary *Roi Fainéant*

Simon Barker

A massive explosion rattles the windows of 10 Downing Street. Cool under fire, the Prime Minister turns inquiringly to his aide, the equally unshakable Cawdor. 'Not one of ours', says Cawdor, a remark which led the *Evening Standard*'s Victor Lewis-Smith to note, with fashionable pessimism, a clear implication that Her Majesty's Government could 'fake an IRA bomb in ninety minutes'.[1] Meanwhile, at the Palace, a sensitive middle-aged Prince has long been engaged in a propaganda war against his estranged wife who lives nearby in 'Sloane Castle'. Points at issue in this tabloid campaign for the hearts and minds of the nation include general moral decay, the widespread poverty experienced in late twentieth-century Britain, ecological farming, private housing and public architecture. The Prince seems also to have successfully endeared himself to the public by means of a recent television broadcast aimed at eclipsing the power of an unpopular Prime Minister, by projecting himself as a more natural leader of a potentially reunited and invigorated kingdom.[2]

In the television drama *To Play the King*, Andrew Davies's acclaimed interpretation of the Michael Dobbs *roman-à-clef*, a sense of the relationship between national identity and constitutional procedure was examined through a generic splicing of Renaissance tragedy and that longest-running of Whitehall farces – Whitehall itself. For Victor Lewis-Smith, searching for a critical methodology suitable for sleepy evening commuters, *To Play the King* (like the earlier series *House of Cards*) 'disproved Marshall McLuhan's definition' and revealed television as the hottest of media – a critical paradigm employed in order to celebrate the uncanny blurring between Dobbs's fiction and the heavily fictive narrative of the 'real' relationship between the monarchy, the state and the press in recent months. The latest episode of this blurring was indeed the recent two and a half-hour television documentary which, even if it did not quite make Charles out to be the kind of disaffected egalitarian of *To Play the King*, certainly helped secure for him a humanitarian agenda at odds with that of the wretched John Major.

To Play the King was a long way from the occasionally unscripted world of Major himself who, when an IRA mortar exploded in his back garden, quite sensibly joined his colleagues under the Cabinet Room's sturdy table. In the real world of Downing Street in the early summer of 1994, my guess is that the question 'is it one of ours?' was more likely to have been asked in the context of Irish World Cup goals rather than Irish bombs, a revisiting of national identity if ever there was one.

But a King Charles as ascending television star? Radio Four's spiritual soundbite, *Thought for the Day*, recently pondered the discontinuity between his 'personality' and his 'profession', and reached new heights of apostasy, if not downright lunacy, by comparing the sensitive Charles with that other personally popular but professionally awkward world leader, Jesus Christ: 'we should remember that "Christ" was not His surname, but His role, the Son of Man'.[3] The real Charles may find more sympathy among Radio Four listeners than with *News At Ten* viewers at present, but there was a striking similarity between his manipulation of the media against the Prime Minister in *To Play the King* and the continuing image-makers' war in which the Prince and the Princess of Wales are engaged.

Critics found the correspondence between this simulated world of high office and the slightly surreal goings-on in the world of John Major's cabinet irresistibly compelling. *To Play the King* was certainly peopled by figures of a pleasing authenticity. There were corrupt newspaper proprietors, toady BBC Director Generals, vapid Princesses, and best of all, the maverick Charles-figure himself, agonising over the discontinuity between the concept of 'nation' and the reality of a severely divided country threatened by an encroaching underclass. Increasingly engaged in a discursive battle with Urquhart over the concept of 'the nation' by means of sound-bites, statistical barrages, photo-opportunities and other items of postmodern paraphernalia, the King was finally defeated and brought to abdication through the rather more concrete means of assassination, phoney kidnap attempts, and the electoral promise of a return to National Service – a trump card which would restore Conservative fantasies of nationhood and, according to Francis Urquhart, might yield a bonus in removing large sections of the underclass to a foreign field from which, with any luck, they would not return. All this was set in a wonderfully stylised simulation of the ministerial and royal realms. Magnificently sparkling interiors were linked by speeding limousines in a kind of hyper-reality which led one normally quite rational colleague to judge the show a success not only because of its display of the 'inner workings of government' but its apparent intrusion into the inner space of Downing Street and the Royal Palaces.

Clearly there is a considerable amount to be said for regarding this kind of critical reaction in terms of the confused response people sometimes make to soap opera: writing to and quoting fictional characters, mistaking fictional situations and locations for real ones, and integrating fictional history with 'real' history. This kind of response, although by no means a recent phenomenon, nor restricted to the electronic media (Charles Dickens was plagued by people in the street enquiring of the health of characters he had invented but was perceived to be 'reporting on' as an ex-journalist), has been seen, of late, as symptomatic of our 'postmodern condition'.[4] But in its pretensions to revelations about the working of power, there is also a parallel to be made between these responses to *House of Cards* and *To Play the King*, and some current characterisations of postmodernity. An example might be Christopher Norris's scathing view that:

> the idea has got around – among 'advanced' thinkers of various political persuasions – that realist epistemologies are a thing of the past; that truth-values in criticism have now been discredited (or shown up as just a figment of bourgeois ideology); that history and politics are textual (= fictive) phenomena on a par with poems, novels or whatever other 'kinds of writing' you care to name; and that henceforth the only 'discourse' that counts is one that cheerfully acknowledges this, along with such *faits accomplis* as the 'deconstruction' of the human subject as a locus of ethical choices, conflicts, and responsibilities.[5]

In fact, a curious connection exists between the critical responses to the dramatisations of Dobbs's novels and the Queen's 1993 *Christmas Message to the Commonwealth*. Having escaped the rebuilding work at Windsor and the post-tourist clearing-up at Buckingham Palace, Her Majesty was, unusually, broadcasting from the library at Sandringham which, as a setting, had a curious *House of Cards/To Play the King* feel about it. The room was a kind of booklined academic inner-space, but was actually dominated by a large television set on which flickered scenes of the outer-world of starvation and disorder recalled from the ebbing year.

Her Christmas musings began, as they often do, with a stab at historical and cultural continuity:

> Most of the books on these shelves date from my Great Grandfather's time and their titles reflect the life and events of those days ... There are many here about war – especially the First World War which ended 75 years ago. Families and loved ones of those who fought in it knew little of the horrors of the trenches other than from artists' drawings and photographs such as these, often published days or weeks after the event. Nowadays stories and pictures from all over the world can be gathered up and appear in print within hours. We have indeed become a global village. It's no longer possible to plead ignorance about what is going on in far-off parts of the world. Switch on the radio or television and the graphic details of events are

instantly available to us. Not all bring gloomy news: the year has seen significant progress made towards solving some of the most difficult problems. The Middle East, for instance, the democratic future of South Africa and most recently Northern Ireland.

A curious set of conflicting allusions operates here. Oddly, searching for a critical methodology suitable for sleepy Christmas viewers, the Queen summoned Marshall McLuhan's concept of the 'Global Village', in much the same way as Victor Lewis-Smith recalled his idea of the 'hot medium'. Clearly McLuhan is back in vogue in some critical circles.

Secondly, she was concerned with the fact that the electronic media conceal as much as they reveal: 'those involved in international charity work confirm that modern communications have helped to bring them support and made them more effective ... but much of their work never reaches the headlines on television.' From the sumptuous setting of Sandringham Castle this may simply have been geared to reminding us of the charity work of her own family – as if to persuade us that in the 'Global Village', her own son is not simply the village idiot.

More interestingly, given the context, it could be said that the power of the monarch lies in the fact that the images of disorder and strife, summoned by means of television from beyond the library, are there to bolster a dazzling display of royal certainty and control, a system of power and reinforcement strikingly similar to that posited by some recent theorists: disorder, and even resistance itself, are perhaps generated by a powerful set of governing interests in order to regenerate power itself. Besides which, wherever there is disorder, especially in a Commonwealth which helps define British nationhood in the contemporary vision of British monarchy, there is also Christian charity, an exacting barometer of the quiet goodwill of the British people.

The Queen's touchstone for the technological advances made by the media over the last 75 years was the set of illustrations from books recording the First World War, which she displayed as an historical curiosity. Although there was a stunning banality about the broadcast, there was at the same time also an almost mischievous critical and political ambivalence about her choice and discussion of text. Was she implying that the television omits as much as it reports and is therefore a medium we should treat with considerable suspicion? Did she consider the national interest to have been better served by the time-lag available to those First World War reporters who notoriously doctored news of the conflict? Or did she see the modern world through 'postmodern' eyes, understanding the Gulf War to have been conducted, as Dick Hebdige believes, 'in a "virtual space" where rival hypothetical scenarios, "realised" as computer simulations, fight it out over the data supplied by satellites', which so contrasts with Christopher Norris's evocation of the:

> experience of soldiers in the First World War, witnessing the horrors and catastrophic setbacks as a matter of brute, self-evident fact, and then reading reports in the British Press – geared entirely to the propaganda effort which falsified the casualty lists, treated the conflict as a tolerably civilized affair, and echoed the standard morale-boosting line that victory was just around the corner.[6]

Postmodernist theory curiously coincides with the pessimism of *House of Cards* and *To Play the King*. There is seemingly no way out of this world of surfaces and simulation. In fact, like Norris's analysis of the Gulf War, history and form have something to tell us about the projection of political power.

House of Cards and *To Play the King* were characterised by their playful but calculated reproduction of some of the commonest tropes of Elizabethan and Jacobean political tragedy. The Prime Minister is soon haunted by the images of those he has clinically removed on his way first to the Premiership and subsequently, in all but name, to the throne itself. His wife is a passable Lady Macbeth, assuring him he will not fail if he screws his courage to the sticking place. Bardic quotations – 'I am in blood steeped in so far' – supply such moment, resonance, and illumination at times of governmental crisis that you begin to wonder exactly why the Tories are so keen to thrust Shakespeare down the throats of children in the name of a national culture. At the end of *To Play the King*, the bodies were piled as deep along the way to power as in any self-respecting early-modern revenge play or Shakespearean History.

A striking reference point in *To Play the King* was indeed Shakespeare's *Richard III*, partly because of the constant re-invention of the protagonist through layers of dissemblance, and partly because of the taxonomy of bestial and monstrous imagery employed used to describe him. For the King's advisors, the 'bottled spider' of the Shakespeare text had become the 'smiling crocodile' of the inhuman Prime Minister Urquhart. The device of direct address to the camera echoed the 'discussion of plans with the audience' device, long-identified with the late-Medieval Vice figure revitalised in Shakespeare's play. Francis Urquhart may be the repellent 'FU', but he also has the sensual attraction of Shakespeare's Richard, a strong and potentially noble figure in a fallen world.

Everyone knows that Shakespeare's play can be seen as a part of the Tudor revisionist project, an essential demonisation of the last of the Plantagenets. But everyone should also know that the play can be read in conjunction with an analysis of Elizabethan *realpolitik* in a way which interrogates the very

69

structures of power and authority exercised by the Tudors themselves. Read in earlier years, particularly in the middle of the twentieth century, as a naturalised ethic of power, *Richard III* has begun recently to yield the uncertainties of that ethic and therefore its considerable vulnerability. At one time the seamless conjunction of 'Tudor Myth' and gilded poetic expression announced for critics an inevitable hierarchy and a cultured historicism which denied the institutional chaos which latter-day critics and historians have produced as a context for the production of tragedy. Everyone knows this was to do with the insecurity of national identity rather than a belief in its universal truth, even if New Historicism comes close to restoring a model of power which suggests quite the opposite.[7]

In fact, if *fin de siècle* comparisons are to be made, then the pessimism of postmodernity seems more like that of those melancholy Elizabethan gentlemen who fled court, city and commonwealth for a cultured country life because they feared comets in the skies over London and the strange beasts seen swimming up the Thames – not to mention the prophecies they read of in each other's books. If the contemporary postmodern intelligentsia is the millennial equivalent of those gloomy late Elizabethans, then it is not surprising to discover equally weak thought masquerading as considered analysis of institutions and power. Examples would be the postmodern observation that all nationalism is meaningless because, as if only yesterday, capitalism has become international. Or the notion that the contemporary impulse towards Cultural Studies within the academic institution *simply* serves the commercialisation of education, which amounts to a discovery of what many knew all along – that what happens in the institution has always been dependent on what happens outside it. As for political activity, we are urged to swim with the tide, rather like those apocalyptic creatures spotted in the Elizabethan Thames, and plan local adjustments or transgressions in the face of an irresistible culture of power. As Christopher Norris has noted, this implies that 'our last best hope as intellectuals is to cultivate the private virtues (compassion, tolerance, a measure of irony with regard to our own pet beliefs) and renounce all those grandiose Enlightenment ideals of setting the world to rights.'[8] Ironically, even the absurd Prince Charles, whom many, if they thought of him at all, would have seen as the contemporary *Roi Fainéant* in the context of the reality of political power in Britain, is crazily to the left of a postmodernism whose majestic stance as King of Theory takes on the more literal meaning of the term – the 'lazy King'.

NOTES

1. Victor Lewis Smith, 'Faultless Tilt at the Throne', in the *Evening Standard*, 13th December 1993.

2. Central T.V., *Charles: The private man, the public role*, 29th June 1994.

3. 'Thought for the Day', *The Today Programme*, BBC Radio Four, 1st July 1994.

4. For a discussion of this phenomenon, see Fredric Jameson, *Postmodernism, or the Cultural Logic of Late Capitalism*, London 1991, 276–7.

5. Christopher Norris, *Uncritical Theory*, London 1992, 52.

6. Dick Hebdige, 'Bombing Logic', *Marxism Today*, March 1991, 46. Christopher Norris, op. cit., 122.

7. For an analysis of the politics of New Historicism, see M. D. Jardine, 'New Historicism for Old: New conservatism for old? The politics of patronage in the Renaissance', in Andrew Gurr, ed., *The Yearbook of English Studies*, London 1991, Vol. 21, 286–304.

8. Christopher Norris, *The Truth About Postmodernism*, Oxford 1993, 278.

9

Class masquerades as nation:
recent films; Don DeLillo; Martin Amis

Richard Kerridge

Discourses of national identity are often discourses of social class in disguise. I want to examine this by looking at three recent films which feature relations between Englishness and Americanness, and at two comic novels about postmodernity, one American and one English. The films are *The Remains of the Day*, *Shadowlands* and *Four Weddings and a Funeral*. The novels are Don DeLillo's *White Noise* and Martin Amis's *London Fields*.[1]

In his essay 'Americanism and Fordism',[2] Antonio Gramsci discussed an attitude to America prevalent on both Left and Right in the Europe of the 1920s. This is an instructive example of an ideology of class masquerading as one of national identity. When European cultural commentators declared that American culture was invading or 'swamping' Europe,[3] with the cultural uniformity imposed by American systems of mass-production, they were, in Gramsci's view, expressing not so much nationalism as class-anxiety that traditional social and cultural hierarchies might be overthrown: 'the problem is rather this: whether America, through the implacable weight of its economic production (and therefore indirectly), will compel or is already compelling Europe to overturn its excessively antiquated economic and social basis'.[4] To put the argument loosely, the Americans, from the point of view of a European cultural élite, signified both the petit-bourgeoisie and the working-classes in their new aspect as mass-consumers. American culture meant commodified popular culture, often regarded as invasive and swamping. Defensive culture-snobbery presented itself as defence of the indigenous. The other side of this equation is that European, particularly British, culture often functions for Americans as a signifier of a lost, defeated, disavowed and longed-for aristocracy.

For Jürgen Habermas, one of the main factors in the crisis of legitimation he discovers in late capitalism is the erosion, by successive waves of social mobility, of the pre-capitalist ideologies on which capitalism depends for part of its legitimation.[5] One such ideology is the notion of natural aristocracy, to which newly-successful groups appeal in order to stabilise and naturalise their new position. In late-capitalist culture, this idea of natural aristocracy is most often used to stabilise relations between an older bourgeoisie and a newly emergent one. Usually the process is represented by love and marriage across class boundaries. The old hierarchy is revitalised through marriage with the new.

In the traditional marriage between old feudalistic aristocracy and emergent bourgeois capitalism, the former is both revitalised and protected by the alliance, while the latter has its new privileges naturalised and legitimated.

A typical 1980s example is the late-eighties Hollywood success *Working Girl* (1988), directed by Mike Nichols. Here a working-class office secretary competes successfully with, and eventually displaces, her supercilious and preppy female boss. The boss, described on the poster as a 'career bitch', is the film's villain. Thus, a reassuringly ingenuous and patronisable version of the career woman is used to defeat a more aggressive and threatening version. And in case even this heroine is too threatening, in terms of gender and class, she is tamed when she falls in love (and forms a business partnership) with a senior male representative of the old order, played by Harrison Ford, who is attracted by her emergent, resourceful vitality. Her rags-to-riches story is revealed not as a challenge to hierarchy, but as a specifically American capitalist myth, a form of legitimation which triumphantly compares meritocratic America to older European cultures based on inert privilege. In the final scene she is shown welcoming her own secretary with a smile, as the film hints that the capitalist structure has been both validated and rendered more humane by her trajectory.

I want to place this relatively simple fable of social mobility in the 1980s alongside three recent films which use national identity – setting American characters against English characters – to represent a similar process. These are the Merchant/Ivory adaptation of Kazuo Ishiguro's novel *The Remains of the Day* (1993), Richard Attenborough's *Shadowlands* (1993) and Mike Newell's extraordinarily successful *Four Weddings and a Funeral* (1994). All three are English-produced films aimed at the mass American market. They all deploy beautiful landscapes and historic stately homes (Oxford colleges function as stately homes in *Shadowlands*). Most significantly, they all position an American character in relation to the English aristocracy, in a way which combines criticism with desire.

In *The Remains of the Day*, a visiting American senator is the most authoritative opponent of the appeasement policies of the English aristocrat Lord Darlington and his circle of fascist-sympathisers. After the war, this American buys Darlington Hall and takes the disgraced Lord Darlington's place as master to the butler, Stevens, the film's central character. Ishiguro's novel has two American characters, the senator who challenges Darlington and a millionaire who buys the hall. In conflating the two, the film emphasises the ambivalence of an American viewpoint which first makes a passionate critique of the British social structure – seen here as compromised, brutal, obsessed with deference and sexually repressed – and then seeks to be admitted to the most compromised part of that structure, the aristocracy.

In *Shadowlands* the pattern is similar. The American poet, Joy Gresham, is attracted by C. S. Lewis's old-fashioned gentlemanliness and repelled by his authoritarianism and self-repression. When she marries him, she gains the sanction of the cultural tradition he represents, while bringing him to emotional life: a typical mythic American-English exchange. In *Four Weddings and a Funeral*, Carrie, the American character, is a journalist working in London for *Vogue* (that is, she is employed to commodify images of aristocratic life). She moves on the fringes of a smart London set regularly seen at society weddings, and has an affair with a man from this group. Her lover, Charles, is played by Hugh Grant, whom the film has established as the latest exponent of sexy English gentlemanliness.[6] Carrie takes the sexual lead from the start, but her real task is to overcome his emotional timidity; precisely the inarticulate, gentlemanly shyness which attracts her. She succeeds in this, but only after the collapse of her first attempt to join an ancient aristocracy – her disastrous marriage to Hamish, who owns a Scottish castle.

In each of these fables, the role of the American character is that of a modern, economically-powerful professional bourgeoisie making its peace with an old aristocracy. Iain Chambers has argued, after Perry Anderson, that Britain, as the first leading industrial nation, never advanced to a fully capitalist culture, since its institutions were always pre-emptively shaped by landed interests and city finance.[7] Until the middle of the twentieth century, this structural condition was masked by the colonial economy. Throughout the industrial-capitalist period, British culture has therefore been dominated by feudalist, organicist legitimations of the social and economic hierarchy, much more than by capitalist-meritocratic legitimations. In contrast, the main legitimating ideologies in America are meritocratic, but meritocratic competition does not offer stable hierarchies, and from these films at least it seems that the British can still function for an American middle-class as a stand-in aristocracy, with which there is desire for alliance.

In Britain, organicist legitimations were given a prolonged life by the forms of national identity constructed during the Second World War, and then by the Welfare State. Meritocratic and free-market ideologies, though always present, did not threaten to become dominant until the 1970s and '80s, when increasing perceptions of national decline coincided with the emergence of a new bourgeoisie detached from the old working-class. For a cultural response to this, and to comparable developments in Reagan's America, I will turn to the two novels, which, in different ways, are concerned with anxieties provoked in the paternalistic *haute-bourgeoisie* by the new majorities and changing cultural values of the 1980s. The purpose of this discussion is to illustrate, again, the function of foreign national identities in signifying systems motivated primarily

74

by class. Specifically, I shall look at the ambivalence and sense of foreignness experienced by that *haute-bourgeoisie* in the face of contemporary popular culture.

Don DeLillo's comic novel *White Noise* shows an American use of Germanness to signify an exiled 'real'.[8] The narrator and central character, Jack Gladney, is head of a university department of Hitler Studies. The world he inhabits is recognisably the contemporary postmodern world as described by Jean Baudrillard. In a culture dominated by the multiple reproduction of images and the rapid commodification of styles, referentiality and the real have been displaced, more than ever before, by *simulacra*: by copies, by narratives which construct subjectivity. Material processes, of production, of the body, of the natural world, are effaced. Nothing is anchored; everything is 'floated' on the market and carried away from its original context, becoming a signifier in someone else's code. The optimistic view of this condition is that everyone becomes mobile, free to borrow from different places, not restrained by any particular context of identity, belief or history. Everyone in this world is a cultural consumer, but every commodity purchased is a simulacrum, detached from its origin, weightless. Culture is turned into style or life-style. But in this culture of weightlessness and consumer-freedom, characters are haunted by repressed knowledge of their own mortality, which becomes an authenticity displaced onto other people thought to have a more authentic way of living. For Jack, the Germans function in this way. He seeks to borrow their authenticity.

The 'age of simulation' comes about through the disappearance of referentiality and the resulting availability of signs as floating signifiers which 'lend themselves to all systems of equivalence, all binary oppositions and all combinatory algebra.'[9] So Jack is free to commodify Hitler; this is a shrewd move in the academic market-place. 'Hitler', as a token in this system of exchange, seems merely equivalent to any other academic topic. One of Jack's colleagues, Murray, plans to establish a similar school of Elvis studies. DeLillo uses the academic world, in which ideas and names, rather than material products, are the commodities, as a defining instance of the postmodern.

For Baudrillard, this floating of signifiers and undermining of cultural and moral fixity is connected with the efforts of governments in the 1980s to create a new cultural majority which would marginalise the poor politically and ghettoise them physically (while commodifying their lives as narratives of danger and authenticity).[10] This new majority is also threatening to the older middle-class and its cultural hierarchies. Jack, as a representative of this class, suppresses any recognition of arbitrariness or lightness when thinking about his own academic appropriations, but is amused and puzzled by such representatives of tabloid culture as Orest Mercator, who wants to break the world record for sitting in a cage of poisonous snakes. What bewilders Jack is Orest's assumption of physical immortality. A commodifier of images of death himself, Jack appeals to the physical real when confronted with alien cultural signifiers.

Jack and Murray are careful to avoid anything so uncool and self-immobilising as the contemporary high-culture jeremiad offered by Allan Bloom in *The Closing of the American Mind*,[11] for example, or by Paul Fussell in *BAD*.[12] Rather, Jack and Murray's technique is to use what Fredric Jameson has called 'blank parody',[13] as a way of creating an implied space of difference from what is described, without establishing this different position as more than a ghostly one. Each is an uninhibited postmodernist consumer, but each at times deploys a bemused sense of the absurdity of other people's signifiers. For Jack, 'there was something touching about the fact that Murray was dressed almost totally in corduroy. I had the feeling that since the age of eleven in his crowded plot of concrete he'd associated this sturdy fabric with higher learning in some impossibly distant and tree-shaded place'.[14] Jack presents himself as a more relaxed, authentic academic who can find the ingenuousness of his arriviste colleague 'touching'. In turn, Murray, the inventor of Elvis studies, declares himself perplexed, almost Allan Bloom-style, by some of his colleagues: 'I understand the music, I understand the movies, I even see how comic books can tell us things. But there are full professors in this place who read nothing but cereal boxes' (10). In his efforts to establish himself, Murray is not above the momentary reintroduction of traditional canonical notions of the valuable and the trivial.

Most importantly, Jack and Murray distance themselves from anyone with a practical knowledge of material processes; that is, from anyone intimately involved with the irreversibility of the material world, of machines and of the body. In the era of simulation, *production* has been concealed or exported. As the United States and British economies are redefined, increasingly, as consumption and service rather than manufacturing economies, foreign national identity tends to be associated with exiled or lost contact with the material. Working-class people have the same signifying function in Jack's code. Early in the novel Murray remarks that 'people who can fix things are usually bigots' (33). These are then identified as people who have plastic charms dangling from their rear-view mirrors. In Jack's life, the embodiment of this ability to fix things – and of blue-collar identity in general – is his father-in-law, Vernon Dickey, who always talks 'about gaskets and washers, about grouting, caulking, spackling. There were times when he seemed to attack me with terms like ratchet drill and whipsaw' (245). The very mention of physical tools seems to be an assault, and Jack always somehow associates Vernon with death, the great repressed 'real' which haunts Jack and haunts the novel. Sitting, unannounced, in the garden, Vernon is mistaken by Jack for the angel of death (243). Shortly afterwards he makes Jack the gift of a revolver.

The idea of the material world functions for Jack as a reminder of his mortality; what is repressed, in the age of simulation, is anything irreversible, anything that cannot be commodified, that pins the self to a particular place and time. The characters in *White Noise* treat the self not as finite and given but as a cultural construction, endlessly redesignable. They are haunted, however, by the spectre of an exiled real, represented for Jack by the poor, the working-classes, the ecological crisis and anything German.

Although he is the inventor of Hitler studies, Jack is only beginning, falteringly, to learn German, and his efforts to control the language bring him to an unexpected reacquaintance with the materiality of his body:

> The German tongue. Fleshy, warped, spit-spraying, purplish and cruel. One eventually had to confront it ... But the basic sounds defeated me, the harsh spurting northernness of the words and syllables, the command delivery. Something happened between the back of my tongue and the roof of my mouth (31).

The German language becomes a physical organ: the German tongue. During one German lesson, the teacher puts his hand into Jack's mouth, to adjust his tongue (173). Jack has named his only son Heinrich, hoping to gain for him the quality of solidity and materiality which contemporary American names apparently cannot bestow:

> I thought it had an authority that might cling to him. I thought it was forceful and impressive and I still do. I wanted to shield him, make him unafraid. People were naming their children Kim, Kelly and Tracy ... There's something about German names, the German language, German *things* (63).

Germanness has these meanings, it would seem, because of the old association with death, deriving from the Holocaust, combined with a newly intensified association of Germanness with efficient high-tech manufacturing.[15] Like the British aristocracy, this latter capacity is both patronised and envied.

In Britain, a key element in Margaret Thatcher's electoral success in the 1980s was the movement of a newly-wealthy section of the working-class away from its traditional labourist culture. These were the famous 'C1s' and 'C2s', otherwise mockingly known as 'Essex Man'. Thatcherite free-market policies often involved attacks upon the culture and institutions of an older middle class – the professionals in education, the health service, the BBC and the law. This older middle class, more at home with the pseudo-aristocratic culture identified by Anderson, tended to be paternalistic rather than populist. In cultural and educational terms, the challenge posed to an old hegemony by an emergent class became the challenge posed by popular culture to the old hierarchical canon.

Martin Amis was associated, in the 1970s and early '80s, with the 'Martian' school of writers, particularly the poets Craig Raine and Christopher Reid. Amis's early novel *Other People* is thoroughly 'Martian' in method. The 'Martian' school was influenced by the anti-modernist Movement group of the 1950s (of which Kingsley Amis was a prominent member), which attempted to identify Englishness as an empiricist, commonsense opposite to the disruptive, internationalist techniques of modernism. Paradoxically, the distinctive feature of the 'Martians' was a reworking of Viktor Shklovsky's Russian Formalist technique of defamiliarisation: making familiar objects and activities seem strange by describing them as if from the point of view of a Martian visitor, an outsider ignorant of their meaning. For the 'Martians' this technique was in part a means of expressing alienation from the contemporary, and particularly from the new dominance of popular culture, without being exposed in explicitly conservative, high-culture stances.

The Martian visitor isn't really a Martian, of course. His otherness is compromised by his use of earthly language: he is a combination of sameness and otherness. In any but the terse poetic forms favoured by Craig Raine, this problem becomes apparent. Therefore, Amis replaces the Martian with a foreign visitor. Indeed, travel writing is in some ways the pe˙fect genre for this stance of ironic marginality, and Amis has also produced a collection of journalistic travel writings on America called *The Moronic Inferno*. In *London Fields*, the ostensible narrator is an American, Samson Young, through whom Amis focuses a passionately ambivalent gaze on the novel's dominant character, Keith Talent. Keith is Essex Man, the new emergent class-figure of the 1980s, made simultaneously into a threatening monster and figure of pathos. Where Baudrillard sees a procession of simulacra, or chain of signifiers, Amis, through Samson Young, describes with satirical horror the emergence of a newly amoral form of capitalism, which he quaintly calls 'cheating':

The other morning Keith had bought five hundred vanity sachets of Outrage, his staple perfume. At lunchtime he discovered that they all contained water, a substance not much less expensive than Outrage, but harder to sell. Keith was relieved that he had already unloaded half the consignment on Damian Noble in the Portobello Road. Then he held Damian's tenners up to the light: they were crude forgeries. He passed on the notes without much trouble, in return for twenty-four bottles of vodka which, it turned out, contained a misty, faintly scented liquid. Outrage! The incident struck Keith as a sign of the times (113).

'Outrage' begins to be a floating signifier, its meaning constantly changing. But whereas in DeLillo the floating of the signifier is disturbing because there is no implied narrative perspective with confidence in real meanings, here the narrator and the implied reader have no doubt that 'Outrage' is not perfume or vodka. The floating of the signifier in postmodern culture is here identified, simply, as 'cheating', and there can only be cheating where there are rules. 'Cheating' has connotations of honour, and of capitalism as a game played by amateurs, regulated by a gentlemanly code rather than by social legislation.

Throughout the novel, the implied reader is assumed to recognise a vocabulary which would be strange to Keith: 'Keith launched into a squalid decameron of recent gallops and tumbles' (154), 'when it came to kissing and telling, Keith was a one-man oral tradition' (167). These are the terms of canonical literary culture, applied ironically to Keith, in a way which distances Keith from any potential reader and reaffirms those canonical cultural values as a reference-point. Interspersed in the narrative are parodies of passages of Joyce and Lawrence. Similarly, whereas both novels make comic play with modern christian names and commercial brand names, the ones Amis uses are not shimmeringly bland like DeLillo's, but crudely disdainful: a character called Pepsi, a drink called *porno*. Amis's negative space is less ghostly, more openly expressive of class disdain and anxiety than DeLillo's, but in both novels the character-narrators, Jack Gladney and Samson Young, are marked out for death. For both, the negative space of ironic observation is a form of non-existence, leading to physical non-existence or the erasure of their class identity. They are caught in an ambivalent position, wanting to affirm their difference from, and sameness to, an emergent class.

NOTES

1.   Don DeLillo, *White Noise*, London 1984; Martin Amis, *London Fields*, London 1989.

2.   Antonio Gramsci, trans. Q. Hoare and G. Nowell Smith, *Selections from Prison Notebooks*, London 1991, 277–318.

3.   ibid., 316–17.

4.   ibid., 317.

5.   Jürgen Habermas, trans. T. McCarthy, *Legitimation Crisis*, Cambridge 1988, 47–8.

6.   It remains to be seen whether this will be damaged or enhanced by the events of summer 1995.

7.   Iain Chambers, *Border Dialogues*, London 1990, 19–21.

8.   The reading of *White Noise* here is indebted to N. H. Reeve and Richard Kerridge, 'Toxic Events: Post-modernism and DeLillo's *White Noise*', *The Cambridge Quarterly*, 23:4 (1994), 303–23.

9.   Jean Baudrillard, ed. Mark Poster, *Selected Writings*, Cambridge 1988, 167.

10.   See Jean Baudrillard, trans. C. Turner, *America*, London 1989, 111–13. See also Dean MacCannell and Juliet Flower MacCannell, 'Social Class in Postmodernity', in C. Rojek and B. Turner, eds., *Forget Baudrillard?*, London 1993, 124–45. The latter argue that postmodern culture is parasitically dependent upon the codes produced by the people it marginalises: 'those in the starkest of human situations'.

11.   Allan Bloom, *The Closing of the American Mind: How higher education has failed democracy and impoverished the lives of today's students*, New York 1987.

12.   Paul Fussell, *BAD or, The Dumbing of America*, New York 1991.

13.   Fredric Jameson, *Postmodernism or, the Cultural Logic of Late Capitalism*, London 1991, 17.

14.   DeLillo, op. cit., 11. Further references are given in the text.

15.   The same association is there, for example, in Tom Wolfe, *The Bonfire of the Vanities*, London 1988, 98, when Sherman McCoy is praying that his Mercedes will get him out of trouble: 'Come on you Krauts, you Panzer heads, you steely-brained machinists ... Do it right'.

10

'We come after': post-Holocaust national identity in recent popular fiction: *Fatherland* and *Eve's Tattoo*

Nicola King

'We come after, and that is the nerve of our condition.'[1] The Holocaust marks a fundamental break in any sense of historical continuity and problematises our sense of what it means to be human – the identity of those who live in any country affected by the Holocaust has been radically affected by this event. The debates around Holocaust memorialisation in Europe and America make it clear that ways of remembering this traumatic historical event are central to post-modern identity formation. Recent fiction has attempted to address this issue in a variety of ways: here I shall suggest readings of two recent novels which have given narrative form to the problematics of British, American and, to some extent, German post-Holocaust national identities.[2] Historically, the Holocaust has raised the question of whether the logic of the project of modernity was such that it ended in the 'rational', bureaucratic and technological slaughter of millions in a bid to eradicate difference, or whether it is better seen as an abandonment of rationality. The former position has been argued most persuasively by Zygmunt Beauman, and that model of 'explanation' of the Holocaust has also been used by theorists of post-modernity as proof of the ending of the Enlightenment project.[3] In the work of Shoshana Felman and Eric L. Santner, who both write persuasively about the processes of mourning, representation and bearing witness after the Holocaust, there is a collapsing of the terms 'post-modern' and 'post-Holocaust' which runs the risk of universalising the Holocaust and using it as 'proof' of particular post-structuralist theories of language and representation.[4] For Felman, 'the cryptic forms of modern narrative and modern art always – whether consciously or not – partake of that historical impossibility of writing a historical narration of the Holocaust, by bearing testimony, through their very cryptic form, to the *radical historical crisis in witnessing* the Holocaust has opened up.'[5]

This impossibility is represented rather differently by those who adopt the irrationalist model of 'explanation': this can result in a mystification of the Holocaust as an eruption of irrational evil which is beyond explanation. This is the case in Ian McEwan's *Black Dogs*, in which the Gestapo's black dogs are used to symbolise this mystified notion of evil which 'will return to haunt us, somewhere in Europe, in another time'.[6]

Felman's 'radical historical crisis of witnessing' is evident also in the realm of the individual; those who have listened to and analysed the testimonies of survivors of the Nazis, who attempted to create 'an event without a witness', attest to a sense of dislocation between the self who suffered and experienced this trauma, and the self who survived it and lives on in the present. Even as apparently confident and reliable a witness as Primo Levi said, 'I myself am not convinced that these things really happened'.[7] Lawrence Langer quotes Charlotte Delbo:

> I have the feeling ... that the 'self' who was in the camp isn't me, isn't the person who is here, opposite you. No, it's too unbelievable. And everything that happened to this other 'self', the one from Auschwitz, doesn't touch me now, *me*, doesn't concern me, so distinct are deep memory ... and common memory.[8]

The Holocaust is an event which 'tests the limits of representation',[9] both for survivors such as Elie Wiesel, who said: 'between the survivor's memory and its reflection in words, his own included, there is an unbridgeable gulf ... A novel about Auschwitz is not a novel, or it is not about Auschwitz',[10] and for those 'who come after'. Adorno's dictum, 'no poetry after Auschwitz', was later qualified by his conclusion that 'literature must resist this verdict' of silence, but almost all those who discuss the limits and ethics of representing the Holocaust in artistic or literary form agree that there is something which resists representation, a gap between word and event which cannot be filled.[11] For Lyotard, there is 'a demand for forms of thinking and writing that do not forget "the fact" of the forgotten and the unrepresentable.'[12] This 'demand' has resulted in a range of post-modern forms of narrative which might seem, on the one hand, to bear witness to this radical break or crisis of representation, whilst on the other, running the danger of relativism or of suggesting that reality is only constructed in discourse. Barbara Foley argues that narratives such as Styron's *Sophie's Choice* are characterised by 'an epistemological relativism that is philosophically akin to the subjectivist attitude towards truth characteristic of the very fascist nightmare they describe.'[13] Martin Amis's *Time's Arrow* is a good example of a novel which provoked this kind of critical disagreement: many condemned it for its use of the Holocaust in demonstrating a clever narrative trick – time runs backwards, so the Jews at Auschwitz are reconstituted out of ashes there instead of being gassed and burned. For Howard Jacobson, on the other hand, 'the trap isn't too little reverence, it's too much': Amis's 'nastiness ... challenges our refinement', producing the sense of release which can only come through blasphemy.[14] Narratives which reverse time or offer counter-factual alternative futures – like Harris's *Fatherland* – do sometimes have the power to shock us out of a sense of over-familiarisation, or of a too-easy identification with the victim – as in Prager's *Eve's Tattoo* – or with the 'good German' – as in (at least) the final stages of Spielberg's film *Schindler's List*.

Post-Holocaust identity is, of course, a particularly painful and troubled issues in Germany. Eric L. Santner, in *Stranded Objects*, uses a psychoanalytic model to describe what he sees as an incomplete process of mourning and residual nostalgia for narcissistic identification and a lost organic community in German culture. The *Historikerstreit* or German Historians' Dispute of the mid- and late 1980s foregrounded once again the question of German national identity, memory and responsibility. Robert Harris's popular novel *Fatherland* makes narrative use of some of the issues raised during the *Historikerstreit* which therefore need some brief explanation here.[15]

In 1985, Ernst Nolte argued that the Nazi extermination camps were not 'original', but copies of Stalin's camps (and also the culmination of a line of development of other, mostly left-wing, forms of terror), and the extermination of the Jews was the result of the perceived threat of Communism from the East, so that it could be called an 'Asiatic deed'. In 1986 Andreas Hillgrüber published *Two Kinds of Ruin: The shattering of the German Reich and the end of European Jewry*. The title makes clear that he is constructing an equivalence between the two, and in fact privileging the shattering of the Reich: two thirds of his essay is concerned with this, and he emphasises an identification with the ordinary soldier fighting on the eastern front without acknowledging that this prolongation of the war also prolonged the extermination of the Jews. Neither deny the Holocaust – as does the British 'historian' David Irving, who also argued in *Hitler's War* that Hitler cannot be held responsible for the killing of the Jews (if indeed it really occurred), as there is no written evidence to prove his knowledge of it. But the attempts of these revisionists to 'normalise' the Holocaust have been interpreted by Habermas and others as part of a project to restore a sense of pride in German national identity and to deny the uniqueness, and even the importance, of the Holocaust.

Fatherland is set in Berlin in 1964: the Berlin that Speer would have built had Germany won the war. The National Socialists are still in power, the Reich has incorporated the whole of Eastern Europe and what was the Soviet Union. The rest of Europe is dominated by Germany in a European Union, and a cold war with the U.S. (under President Joseph Kennedy) is about to come to an end, as a visit from Kennedy is planned to coincide with the Fuhrer's – Hitler's – seventy-fifth birthday. The surface detail of this alternative Germany is very close to that of Orwell's *1984*: carefully orchestrated propaganda, constant war on the Eastern front, adoration of the leader, children trained to betray their parents if necessary, even down to the smell of cabbage in the flats where the hero lives. In a sense, this world seems frighteningly normal, and part of the novel's power to shock is to make us realise how 'normal' or ordinary a stabilised Nazi Germany-dominated Europe might have come to seem: what we have were is the normalisation or banality of evil rather than its mystification. Rebellious youth read Orwell's *1984* and try to listen to the banned Beatles – much as teenagers did in the former GDR. In this way, Harris is suggesting an equivalence between 'totalitarian' states of the left and right, an equivalence also suggested in most readings of *1984*, and also, of course, by Nolte. This link is made clearer when we are told about half way through the novel that, after the war, the Germans gradually discovered the mass graves of the victims of Stalin: all of these are now preserved as:

> memorials to the dead, museums of Bolshevik evil. Children were taken round them; ex-prisoners acted as guides. There was a whole school of historical studies devoted to investigating the crimes of communism. Television showed documentaries on Stalin's holocaust – bleached skulls and walking skeletons, bulldozed corpses and the earth-caked rags of women and children bound with wire and shot in the back of the neck.[16]

This is one of the moments when the text creates a sudden shock of defamiliarisation: we have seen these documentaries about the *Nazi* holocaust, and the truth about crimes committed in the name of communism is only gradually emerging. The plot of *Fatherland* hinges on the fact that as far as the Gestapo are aware, all evidence of the extermination of the Jews has been destroyed, and nobody really knows what happened to the Jews except that they were 'sent east'. This is a counter-factual world in which the promise of Himmler to SS officers in Poznan in October 1943 has been realised: '[t]his is a page of glory in our history which has never to be written and is never to be written.' The claim of the SS officer quoted in Levi's *The Drowned and the Saved* has come true:

> However this war may end, we have won the war against you; none of you will be left to bear witness, but even if someone were to survive, the world would not believe him. There will perhaps be suspicions, discussions, research by historians, but there will be no certainties, because we will destroy the evidence together with you. And even if some proof should remain and some of you survive, people will say that the events you describe are too monstrous to be believed: they will say that they are exaggerations

of Allied propaganda and will believe us, who will deny everything, and not you. We will be the ones to dictate the history of the Lagers.[17]

The SS officer chillingly foresees the Holocaust denial which Harris's novel also in a sense represents: here the Holocaust really is the 'cultural secret' which Soshana Felman claims it is, an 'event without a witness'. The narrative also creates the process of the discovery of the truth, of the forgotten event, for the reader: it begins with the discovery of a body (which turns out to be that of an SS officer) in a lake near Berlin, which is linked by the detective investigating the case to the deaths or disappearances of other SS officers. At first, March, the detective, thinks they were involved in smuggling art treasures out of the Reich into banks in neutral Switzerland: long after he has been officially taken off the case by the Gestapo, he discovers that they had all been present at a conference called by Richard Heydrich in January 1942, at a villa in Wannsee – which we know of as the Wannsee Conference where the Final Solution was planned. From a bank vault in Switzerland he traces an attaché case which contains the documents which provide evidence for the final solution, which four of the participants had agreed to keep and hide away. They were the ones who had to put Hitler's wishes into practice but were worried about the presence of a written order from the Fuhrer – the very absence of which allowed Irving to argue away any responsibility on the part of Hitler. If Germany had lost the war, the participants could have been tried as war criminals (as many, including Eichmann who kept the minutes of the Wannsee conference, actually were) – the existence of the hidden documents could have then been used as proof that they disapproved and wanted to expose the truth. Luther, the last 'survivor', had wanted to trade the documents with the young American journalist who is helping March in exchange for her help in defecting. The Gestapo is desperate to prevent their discovery because it would threaten the new *détente* with the U.S. Amongst the documents, together with the minutes of the Wannsee conference, railway timetables to and from the campus, orders for gas, and the report of a visit to Auschwitz, is a report of a conversation which took place in 1938 between Joseph Kennedy, then ambassador to the United Kingdom, and the German ambassador, in which Kennedy stated that: 'he himself understood the Jewish policy completely ... very strong anti-Semitic tendencies existed in the U.S. and a large portion of the population had an understanding of the German attitude towards the Jews.'[18] The 'Author's Note' at the end of the book tells us that this document is authentic. It again produces the shock of defamiliarisation as it reminds us that anti-Semitism was not a uniquely German phenomenon, of the policy of appeasement, and of the reluctance of the United States and the United Kingdom to admit Jewish refuges (in spite of Kenneth Baker's claim as

Home Secretary when the recent Refugee Act was passed that Britain had been a safe haven for Jews during the war). Charlotte, the American journalist, tells March there is a general suspicion in the U.S. that the Jews might have been killed, but that most people do not care. As they are reading the documents, March suddenly asks her whether anyone will believe it. She is sure that they will, because they will have the facts: we know that 'having the facts' does not prevent neo-fascist Holocaust denial. But, as Charlotte says, even if people deny it, it will 'still be a response to something which existed.'[19]

Their plan is to get the documents out of Germany: Charlotte drives south to Switzerland while March, foolishly, goes to say goodbye to his son, who informs on him to the Gestapo. Whilst he is being tortured he spits the names – Auschwitz, Sobibor, Birkenau – in the face of his torturer (an ex-camp guard) who says, echoing Levi's SS officer: 'they're just names. There's nothing there anymore, not even a brick. Nobody will ever believe it. And shall I tell you something? Part of you can't believe it either.'[20] He is allowed to escape in the hope that he will lead them to Charlotte and the documents: instead he leads them east, following a map which was included with the documentary evidence, to the site of Auschwitz. The novel ends with him finding his evidence – some pieces of reddish brick, half-obscured in the undergrowth – before he goes into the woods to shoot himself before he can be recaptured. Charlotte, by this time will be well over the border and on her way to the United States where the truth will be revealed: the question of American response is left open. The description of the site of Auschwitz evokes the current debate about exactly how to preserve or restore the site, and the wasteland in Lanzmann's *Shoah* which was once the camp Chelmno. The detective thus finds what he did not know he was looking for: the narrative represents a kind of unconscious search for a truth which was always already known.

This popular novel thus makes concrete the fact that history is written by the victors: however, this novel was itself written 'by the victors', and, it might be argued, could also be read as a contribution to the xenophobic anti-German sensibility expressed not so long ago by Nicholas Ridley, or at least to the complacency of seeing the recent wave of racist violence as a German, not a British problem. The reminder of anti-Semitism in the United States and, by implication, in the United Kingdom, and the fact that Britain is an ally of fascist Germany in the text, work against this reading, however. *Fatherland* is a novel which forces us to rethink our (British) sense of post-war, post-Holocaust and 'contemporary' identity in the light of a history which might easily have been very different.

I want to read Prager's *Eve's Tattoo* against an account of a visit to the U.S. Holocaust Memorial Museum by Philip Gourevitch, a first-generation American

whose parents were Jewish refugees and many of whose family were killed by
the Nazis, in order to highlight the debate over how the Holocaust might be
adequately or appropriately memorialised and its victims remembered without
re-victimisation, and to raise the question of post-Holocaust American national
identity. As visitors enter the museum, the first thing they see – to reassure them
of their country's 'innocence' – is George Washington's statement engraved on
a wall: 'The government of the United States ... gives to bigotry no sanction, to
persecution no assistance.' Gourevitch describes the concept of the recently-
opened 'interactive' museum:

> To draw people into this strange new American civics lesson, exhibition
> designers have designed a gimmick for audience participation in the
> Holocaust narrative. Upon admission, visitors are issued with an identity card
> – matched to their age and gender – imprinted with the name and vital
> statistics of an actual Holocaust victim or survivor. As they pass through the
> three floors of the museum's permanent exhibition, museum-goers can push
> these bar-coded cards into computerised stations and measure their progress
> against the fate of their phantom surrogates, most of whom were murdered.[21]

The sample I.D. card sent with the promotional material for the museum is
that of a young Polish boy who wrote to Eleanor Roosevelt telling her that he
was longing to come to America: as Gourevitch points out, 'it is no accident that
the [card] selected for publicity purposes should tell the story of a man described
as having converted from Judaism to Americanism before his death at the hands
of Nazi collaborators.'[22] In Prager's novel, an American journalist called Eve has
the number of an Auschwitz prisoner tattooed on her arm, after having found a
photograph of this woman holding up her arm to the camera amongst her lover's
possessions. She has become obsessed with the history of the Third Reich and
uses the tattoo as a way of telling the stories – at dinner parties, in the vet's
waiting room, at her Smokers Anonymous meeting – of a series of women, all
of whom she calls Eva, who suffered or died at the hands of the Nazis. Prager
credits Claudia Koonz's book *Mothers in the Fatherland* for much of her
material, and the novel is an attempt in narrative to explore what Koonz explores
historically, the reasons why women became Nazis or supported the Nazi
movement when Nazi ideology reinforced absolute sexual difference and,
initially at least, the relegation of women to the home.[23] Prager more or less
reduces Koonz's complex researches into the crude observation that Hitler had
his hand in every German woman's knickers. The novel does attempt to deal
with the question of how the Holocaust might be remembered in individual ways
when most victims have nothing by which to commemorate them and when all

survivors will be dead within the next fifteen years or so, but the novel is embarrassingly over-determined and sentimental: any critical distance between the third-person narration of the novel and the actions and motives of Eve is hard to detect. However, when she tells her stories her own voice gradually disappears and a more neutral, factual narrative voice takes over, an appropriate and even sometimes moving one for the narration of the stories of the victims. But the novel obviously enacts a double appropriation: by the novelist herself, who in the end resolves the conflict between Eve and her lover (who she discovers in the Jewish son of 'catcher' parents, and who could not make love to Eve whilst she had the tattoo) by an accident which conveniently breaks Eve's arm exactly where the tattoo is, Eve's realisation of her own anti-Semitism, and a romantic and sexual reconciliation whilst she is lying badly injured in hospital – and of course by Eve, who gradually becomes 'taken over' by Eva, whose memory she is determined to preserve. The action takes place in 1989: Eve spends much of her time watching news footage of the crumbling of the Berlin Wall, voicing reflections such as: 'look at the determination on their faces, the energy. I wish we felt that here, don't you? ... This makes me feel bad about America, about the hopelessness we've been feeling.'[24] The critique of American society doesn't get much further than this: apart from a brief incident when a homeless black man is beaten up in the street, and the general ignorance or indifference of most of Eve's circle to the Holocaust (although in most cases they only have to be told one of these stories to become aware and sensitised), the novel fails to address American racism, preferring to appropriate an 'other' racism for the appeasement of its guilt. As Gourevitch points out, it is simpler for a culture to build a monument against an absolute evil than to decide what it wants to stand for, and to face more problematic issues about its own identity: 'at a time when Americans seem to lack the confidence to build national monuments to their ideas of good' (although it is hard to imagine what these might be) 'the Holocaust has been seized upon as an opportunity to build instead a monument against absolute evil.'[25] Both Prager's novel and the Holocaust Memorial Museum invite a simple identification with the victim (Gourevitch describes how the visitor is initially also invited to identify with the American 'heroes' who liberated Dachau, and also with the bystander, indifferent or powerless to intervene) and, to some extent, appropriate the Holocaust for their own ends. Many of the stories Eve tells are not those of Jewish women but of Christians, sometimes nurses or gynaecologists, or others who resisted in various ways but who ended up in Auschwitz, and the question of identification with the victim is in fact problematised when the 'real' Eva turns out to be a Nazi supporter whose sons had joined an anti-Nazi youth group: the boys are caught and hanged and their mother turns on an SS officer with her kitchen knife. But in this way women in general, and not the Jews, are constructed as the victims of the Nazis, contributing to what has been called a 'de-Judaising' of the Holocaust – although Prager does expose some of the contradictions in Nazi sexual ideology, and the link between racial and sexual ideologies, along the way. Gourevitch is critical of the museum's invitation to identify with the victims of the Holocaust; as he says:

> the political choices that I face in my life are not those of the Holocaust; nor are the crises of America shown in this museum. If that should change, and I should find myself in the shoes of any of these brutalised people whose stories surround me, nothing I could learn from having studied their plight would help me. I would try not to wind up at the edge of a pit looking down at the corpses whose number I was about to join, but I might wind up there, along the way, I hope I would try to help others, but I might not have the wherewithal and I might not succeed.[26]

As Gourevitch leaves the museum and walks along the Mall, he finds the discarded identity cards in litter bins along the way, bearing the names and numbers of those who died fifty years ago, and who seem to have been killed twice more, once as the visitor follows their path and their fate through the museum, and again as their card is thrown away like so much rubbish after the visit. Eve's narratives, and the stories of the victims whose identities the visitors to the Holocaust Museum are invited to assume, recycle their sufferings – doubtless with the best of intentions – for our edification and entertainment. As Gourevitch describes it, 'there, just off the National Mall in Washington, the victims of Nazism will be on view for the American public, stripped, herded into ditches, shot, buried, and then the tape will repeat and they will be herded into ditches again, shot again, buried again'.[27] There is probably no 'right' way to commemorate or memorialise events such as these, which is not an argument that they should not be memorialised at all. James Young has written about the 'anti-monuments' in Germany, which, like some post-modern narratives, attempt to represent the gaps and silences, the very impossibility of memorialisation.[28] And the Museum of Tolerance attempts to place the Holocaust in the context of other kinds of American racism. It has often been commented upon that there is no Museum of Slavery in the U.S., nor any plan to build one, although a Museum of African-American History is planned. This omission could be read either as a refusal to give public acknowledgement of American guilt or as a decision not to represent African-Americans solely as victims, as are the Jews in the Holocaust Museum. The images and representations offered by this museum and by writers such as Prager also ignore the massive sense of dislocation caused by the experience, for victims and survivors as well as for those who attempt to realise it later. As Levi said: '[w]e, the survivors, are not the true witnesses ... We speak in their stead, by proxy'.[29] If Levi was aware of this, how much more so should we be, as those 'who come after'.

NOTES

1.   George Steiner, *Language and Silence*, London 1992.

2.   Robert Harris, *Fatherland*, London 1992; Emily Prager, *Eve's Tattoo*, London 1992.

3.   Zygmunt Beauman, *Modernity and the Holocaust*, Cambridge 1991.

4.   Shoshana Felman and Dori Laub, *Testimony: Crises of witnessing in literature, psychoanalysis and history*, New York 1992; Eric L. Santner, *Stranded Objects: Mourning, memory, and film in postwar Germany*, Ithaca 1990.

5.   Felman and Laub, op. cit., 201.

6.   Ian McEwan, *Black Dogs*, London 1992, 174.

7.   Primo Levi, *If This is A Man*, London 1987, 109.

8.   Lawrence Langer, *Holocaust Testimonies: The ruins of memory*, New Haven 1992, 5.

9.   The phrase is adapted from the title of Saul Friedlander, ed., *Probing the Limits of Representation: Nazism and the 'Final Solution'*, Cambridge, Mass. 1992.

10.   Elie Wiesel, 'A Plea for the Survivors', in *A Jew Today*, New York 1978, 234.

11.   Quoted by Felman in Felman and Laub, op. cit., 34.

12.   David Carroll, 'Foreword', to Jean-Francois Lyotard, *Heidegger and 'the Jews'*, Minneapolis 1990, xiii.

13. Barbara Foley, 'Fact, Fiction, Fascism: Testimony and mimesis in Holocaust narratives', *Comparative Literature*, 32 (1982), 358.

14. Howard Jacobson, 'Jacobson's List', *The Independent*, 2nd February 1994, 19.

15. For a detailed account, see Charles S. Maier, *The Unmasterable Past: History, Holocaust, and German national identity*, Cambridge, Mass. 1988.

16. Harris, op. cit., 211–12.

17. Primo Levi, *The Drowned and The Saved*, London 1988, 1: quoted by Harris, op. cit., 329.

18. Harris, op. cit., 309–10.

19. ibid., 335.

20. ibid., 364.

21. Philip Gourevitch, 'In the Holocaust Theme Park', *The Observer Magazine*, 30th January 1994, 20.

22. ibid., 22.

23. Claudia Koonz, *Mothers in the Fatherland: Women, the family and Nazi politics*, London 1987.

24. Prager, op. cit., 39.

25. Gourevitch, op. cit., 25.

26. ibid., 24.

27. ibid., 25.

28. James E. Young, *The Texture of Memory: Holocaust memorials and meaning*, New Haven 1993.

29.   Primo Levi, *The Drowned and The Saved*, 63–4.

11

Dates and infidelities:
Ford Madox Ford and national history

Colin Edwards

Although he fought for the Allied cause during the Great War, it was not until 1919 that 'Ford Madox *Hueffer*' dropped his German surname in favour of 'Ford Madox Ford'. Ironically, Ford was about as 'quintessentially English' in his demeanour as Christopher Tietjens, the central character in *Parade's End*, his novel-sequence of the Great War (this particular patronym – Tietjens – being of High Dutch origins).

Wyndham Lewis recalled the exaggeratedly 'English' mannerisms of an 'omniscient, bored, sleepy Ford' in the first days of August 1914. This was at an aristocratic house-party just over the Scottish border, at Berwick, when Ford, 'in his faintest voice', and 'with consummate indifference', answered his disbelieving fellow-guests, that: '[i]t has always been the Liberals who have gone to war. It is *because* it is a Liberal Government that it *will* declare war'.[1]

Ford's negligence about precise dates (sometimes it is the third, at other times the fourth of August when the German army crossed the border into France) is as noteworthy as his prescience concerning this particular event. Ford, like many other commentators on the period, was haunted by the coincidence of private events with the grand moments of national crisis or celebration. Christopher Tietjens, who in 1916 is about to return to his Welch regiment in France, struggles against the effects of shell-shock before he can recall the place-name (and Ford chooses to make it Berwick) from which he travelled back to London on the eve of the war. His baffled mind eventually draws upon the associations of private memory to reconstruct how he had rescued his friend, Macmaster, from the social disgraces attached to intra-marital infidelity:

> Macmaster had said that he dare not travel with Mrs Duchemin because all London would be going south by that train. All London had. It pushed in at every conceivable and inconceivable station all down the line – it was the great rout of the 3–8–14 [3rd August,1914].[2]

Tietjens, as is his wont, does the decent thing: *he* takes the rap as 'all London' crosses the border into England: 'Tietjens had got on board at Berwick, where they were adding extra coaches, and by giving a £5 note to the guard ... had got a locked carriage. It hadn't remained locked for long enough.'

What I wish to call attention to here is Ford's fascination with the large events by which national history is marked out, and the common ground which they share with individuals' inner histories. More significant to my argument is the fact that *both* forms of history (private and public) are fictionally constructed around the idea of *infidelity*.

A number of critics – perhaps most recently, James Scott – have disputed Ford's much better-known use of the historical date (this time *4th* August, 1914) in *The Good Soldier*.[3] The date, recurring across this fiction, is here associated with private catastrophe and deceit. Florence Hurlbird's marriage with John Dowell and her suicide (because of the 'good soldier', Ashburnham's, infidelity), are only two of the fictional events falling on that fateful day. John Dowell, who narrates the novel in the first-person, speaks of this notable signifier in the following terms: 'I do not know whether that is one of those sinister, as if half-jocular and altogether *merciless* proceedings on the part of a cruel Providence that we call coincidence.'[4] This ironic use of coincidence seems to establish history itself as the anonymous, 'merciless' onlooker to the sphere of private events in *The Good Soldier*. Like an inhuman judge watching the arena of human failings, Ford includes this impersonal cypher of authority inside a novel, however, which is actually slow to prescribe judgements upon its various victims.

John Dowell never pretends to objectivity: his method is one of continual return and revisit (a strongly Fordian word), as he tries to get the past into some kind of perspective. Dowell draws attention to his particular brand of Impressionism (just as Conrad's Marlow does in *Heart of Darkness*):

> No, we never did go back anywhere. Not to Heidelberg, not to Hamelin, not to Verona, not to Mont Majour – not so much as to Carcassone itself. We talked of it, of course, but I guess Florence got all she wanted out of one look at a place. She had the seeing eye.[5]

Himself lacking the 'seeing eye', Dowell's narrative method should not be too closely identified, perhaps, with the influential tenet of Joseph Conrad (and to some extent, of Ford) when writing about the aims of his fiction: '[i]t is, before all, to make you *see*'[6]. Or perhaps it is in the area of difficulty about 'seeing' to the heart of any historical problem, where I would wish to locate the interest of Ford's individual approach to the 'truth' of any past event, and for that matter, of his approach to national histories.

1913, a year in which Ford and his mistress, the novelist Violet Hunt, had been dragged through the law-courts by Ford's wife, Elsie Hueffer, was mostly spent away from England, writing drafts of *The Good Soldier* and finishing a study of Henry James.[7] At one point in September 1913 (as Violet Hunt reports in *I Have This To Say, The Story of My Flurried Years*), they had spent a day with C. F. G. Masterman, the Liberal Cabinet Minister, and his wife Lucy, weaving unsteadily across former Franco-Prussian battlefields: 'a line of frontier like a wriggling snake,whose every convolution would take up about a hundred yards.'[8] They were being shadowed by German officials, whom Violet thought mistook Masterman for Winston Churchill.

It is a nicely symbolic cameo of Ford at this time that is given by Violet: with these four tourists (doubling momentarily for the four tourists – Dowell and Florence, the 'good soldier' Ashburnham and Leonora perhaps?) erratically criss-crossing a borderline of Ford Hueffer's other homeland, unconscious of the future significance of this terrible borderline of nations:

> [the driver] did it very funnily, in order to plague us – driving like a snail over German territory, and whipping up his horse and shaking us to bits when we happened to be on French. We held the map on our knees and roared with laughter.[9]

The situation might well have appealed to the novelist in Ford, as they were driving over 'every mound' (to quote again from Violet's memoirs) 'in which a German's body lay': '[t]hat, you know, is what life really is – a series of such meaningless episodes beneath the shadow of doom – or of impending bliss, if you prefer it.'[10] Ford had also written in his famous *English Review* editorials of 1909 (republished as *The Critical Attitude*) that it was the special virtue of Henry James and of Joseph Conrad to: '[take] in hand an 'affair' – a parcel of life, that is to say, in which several human beings are involved – and each having taken hold never loosens his grip until all that can possibly be extracted from the human situation is squeezed out.'[11]

Clearly, Ford describes here the sort of artistic project he was to attempt three or four years later on in *The Good Soldier*. Again, the emphasis falls on the notion of the novelist's *merciless* grip on his fictional situation. Ford seems to use his critical writing of these years (1910 to 1914) to enjoin upon the novelist the task of 'rendering' 'our terrific, untidy, indifferent, empirical age where not one single problem is solved and not one single Accepted Idea from the past has any more magic.'[12] These years, 1910–1914, were certainly Ford's most 'terrible' – for Violet Hunt, the most 'flurried' – years, and also those which provided the most fruitful experience for his future writing of fiction.

But did Ford really come to believe that it was always the duty of the writer to cultivate a kind of Jamesian aloofness, especially when dealing with the subject-matter of the English? Was it, for Ford, a novelist's task always to 'bestow his sympathies [as he wrote of James] upon no cause, [and to remain] an observer, passionless and pitiless[?]'[13] In Henry James' own letters to Violet Hunt at the time of the 'Hueffer scandal' (in 1909), we can catch the accent of his scrupulous (if not frigid) detachment towards Violet at this time. He wrote that he found the situation she had put herself and Ford in as:

> painfully unedifying, and that compels me to regard all agreeable or unembarrassed communication between us as impossible. I can neither suffer you to come down to hear me utter those homely truths, nor pretend at such a time to free or natural discourse of other things on a basis of avoidance of what must now be most to the front in your own consciousness, or what in a very unwelcome fashion disconcerts mine.[14]

Yet, from the evidence of a slightly later letter, it is clear that James is quite as much fascinated as he is repelled by Violet's transgression: 'I didn't forbid you my house; but deprecated the idea of what would otherwise have been so interesting and welcome a *tête a tête* with you.'[15] It becomes clear, indeed, that Ford's own difficult relations with James – and indeed with Joseph Conrad – in his years with *The English Review* (1908–1910) are associated (ironically enough) with the areas of constraint and of tactical silence in the English which, as outsiders, Ford knew they were particularly well-placed to notice.

However, in *The Spirit of the People*, the third volume of his own earlier trilogy written about the English,[16] Ford had actually put his finger on the triumphant English faculty of, as he wrote, 'ignoring the most terrible of facts'; they were (as David Trotter has written on Ford) the 'least apocalyptic people on earth', who prescribed a 'self-suppression at once admirable and terrible'.[17] Indeed, in *The Spirit of the People*, Ford had supplied himself with the bare bones of one of *The Good Soldier*'s culminating moments, when Ashburnham and his young ward, Nancy (each aware of the mutual passion they have for each other) bid farewell to each other for good:

> [t]he train came in ... There was upon those people's faces no expression of any kind whatever. The signal for the train's departure was a very bright red; that is about as passionate a statement as I can get into that scene.[18]

This is a moment where the voice of the conscious craftsman seems to become particularly visible in the novel, expressing itself in the tongue of the New-Englander, John Dowell. As a witness to this most humdrum, or anti-apocalyptic, prelude to Ashburnham's suicide and Nancy's psychosis, Dowell is imaginatively, if not morally, in thrall to the English setting: an exile, he is, as he says, 'that absurd figure, an American millionaire, who has bought one of the ancient haunts of English peace'.[19] Dowell is in the uncomfortable position of living on either side of national frontiers: only marginally can he participate in what was to become the *grand guignol* of the English Country House Party, *circa* 1914.

Dowell is also an 'outsider' insofar as he takes the position of Impressionist: he revisits the past scene (at which he had been physically present), but his narrative's position of retrospect gives him an insight – if a speculative one – into what might have been going on in the mind of the English Captain Ashburnham. The imaginative act of revisiting past history is tense with the force of withheld knowledge.

Looking back to 1913, Violet Hunt refers to the writing of *The Good Soldier*: 'it was going to contain something quite unusual for him; there would be "heart" in it. I was writing one of my novels, too, in which he always said there was *too much* heart – that is to say, sentiment.'[20] Of course, it is Florence in this novel who 'has a heart' (who in fact fakes a heart-condition, in the other sense of the phrase) in order to avoid sexual contact with her husband, John Dowell, so freeing herself for extra-marital affairs. As Dowell goes over the ground of the past, it is as if he can only unlock the pain in his own heart via a series of convolutions in the narrative: by revisiting the mendacities of Florence and of the English 'good soldier', but without the 'seeing eye' of Florence. For him, the truth of any past event can only be disclosed by a journey of traversing and re-traversing: in one sense, it is as if the clue to his fictional discoveries is that the past always remains somewhat uncertain, *difficult*, open to fresh interpretation.

'When one discusses an affair – a long, sad affair – one goes back, one goes forward,' says Dowell, now that the dust *seems* to have settled.[21] In the position of 'exile' that Dowell has occupied in a singularly heart*less* homeland, he is still governed by a sort of fascination with Englishness, and with the 'good soldier'. He is not the sort of merciless, Jamesian outsider that Ford had written of when he once referred to the novelist as a kind of 'stern scientist'.[22]

After the opening of hostilities in 1914 – when War was a settled fact – Ford busied himself very quickly in writing two books of analysis of the French and Prussian temperaments and cultures.[23] In a chapter from *Between St Dennis and St George* (1915) entitled 'The Limits of Honest Criticism', he returned to the subject of the status of historical 'fact', and the particular example of the opening of international hostilities:

> the public should place no credence whatever in a writer writing controver-
> sially upon such matters as the origin of a war unless either in footnotes or

in the text the exact references are given for the authority of statements of fact and the exact quotation of speeches and of written documents.[24]

This concern with the authority of History suggests a rather different 'Ford Madox Ford', it would seem, from the version of Ford as habitual liar, lazy anecdotalist and *raconteur*, that has pursued his literary, and to some extent critical, reputation since his Edwardian heyday, and its nemesis at the time of the divorce scandal.

For Henry James, as we know from his letters from 1914, the coming of war – 'the plunge of civilisation into this abyss of blood and darkness' – reveals his sense of an historical record of apocalyptic treachery: 'to have to take it all now for what the treacherous years were all the while really making for and meaning is too tragic for any words.'[25] But Ford's sense of history – because it is understood in a closer relationship to his understanding of people – aspires to avoid any such 'plunges' of the soul towards either the extreme of apocalyptic despair in the face of crisis, or, on the contrary, towards the inert, apparently indifferent response which he had diagnosed – in fiction and criticism – as one aspect of the English character.

In many ways, John Dowell is a particularly personal character-construction for Ford. There is an implicit fascination with this New-Englander whose 'revisit' to a traumatic past is a new measuring of the boundaries separating himself off from the England he buys into. He senses (rather than clearly sees) the borderlines which demarcate its civilities and its mendacities. He is not – clearly – to be identified precisely with Ford himself, and yet it turns out that he shares with Ford the conviction that he is a sort of exile. Ford's creative writing at this time of extreme personal pressure was following the contours of his critical appreciation with an intriguing closeness: undoubtedly there is a symbiosis of the fictional John Dowell (of 1915) and Ford's critical construction of a 'Henry James' in 1913. The former is in many ways a searching enquiry into the *impasse* and the *nemesis* of the European mind of 1914: John Dowell, cuckolded and abandoned by the European society he has entered, is a detached outsider, and yet also a personal witness to the disintegration of all contracts binding together a whole society. He is in a position to view his own situation from a vantage point which, simultaneously, lends the 'mercilessness' of the Jamesian perspective, and yet also the insight which counts the human costs. Ford's 'Henry James' was only a first stage for Ford, towards giving a full response to this critical moment in history.

Ford was to emerge from the experience of active service in the War with a very positive sense of what it meant for him to be an exile. As Ford was to write much later, in the 1930s, there were advantages in adopting a transnational (in the 1920s a markedly transatlantic) lifestyle:

> [t]here remained in my subconsciousness a conviction that must have grown stronger – that I was not English. Not English at all, not merely 'not really English'. I never had much sense of nationality. Wherever there were creative artists was my country.[26]

So that when we see *Parade's End*'s Christopher Tietjens – often observed to be Ford's archetypal Englishman – distracting his mind from enemy bombardment, in 1916, by composing English sonnets; when we see him on the train, on 3rd August 1914, crossing the Scottish borderline and getting caught up in someone else's romantic and sexual affairs, it would be rash to presume that Tietjens is being constructed as some kind of ideal form of 'Englishness': the trajectory of the whole Tietjens tetralogy is rather towards the averagely carnal man, or, Ford's *'homme moyen sensuel'*.[27] After all, we are told that Tietjens has elected 'to be peculiarly English in habits and in *as much of his temperament as he could control'*.[28]

Ford found it too complicated an affair to see clear boundaries and unpromiscuous borderlines, when he thought both about matters of the heart and of the history of a nation.

NOTES

1. Wyndham Lewis, *Blasting and Bombardiering*, London 1982, 59.

2. Ford Madox Ford, *Parade's End (Some Do Not...)*, New York 1972, 229.

3. James Scott, 'Coincidence or Irony? Ford's use of August 4th in *The Good Soldier*', *English Language Notes*, 30:4 (1993), 53–8.

4. Ford Madox Ford, *The Good Soldier, A Tale of Passion*, Harmondsworth 1987, 75.

5. ibid., 20.

6. Joseph Conrad, 'Preface', *The Nigger of the 'Narcissus'*, Harmondsworth 1989, xlix.

7. Arthur Mizener, *The Saddest Story, A Biography of Ford Madox Ford*, London 1971, 223–57.

8. Violet Hunt, *I Have This To Say, The Story of My Flurried Years*, New York 1926, 248.

9. ibid., 248.

10. Ford Madox Ford, *Henry James*, London 1913, 154.

11. Ford Madox Ford, *The Critical Attitude*, London 1911, 89.

12. Richard M. Ludwig, ed., *The Letters of Ford Madox Ford*, New Jersey 1965, 55.

13. Ford, *Henry James*, 24.

14. Hunt, op. cit., 95–6.

15. ibid., 96.

16. Ford Madox Ford, *The Soul of London*, London 1905; *The Heart of the Country*, London 1906; *The Spirit of the People*, London 1907.

17. Ford, *The Spirit of the People*, 92; David Trotter, 'Hueffer's Englishness', *Agenda*, 27:4 and 28:1 (Winter 1989/Spring 1990), 148–55.

18. Ford, *The Good Soldier*, 224.

19. ibid., 227.

20. Hunt, op. cit., 241.

21. Ford, *The Good Soldier*, 167.

22. Ford, *The Critical Attitude*, 105.

23. Ford Madox Ford, *When Blood Is Their Argument*, London 1915; *Between St Dennis and St George*, London 1915.

24.   Ford, *Between St Denis and St George*, 28.

25.   Cited in Robert Green, *Ford Madox Ford, Prose and Politics*, Cambridge 1981.

26.   Ford Madox Ford, *It Was The Nightingale*, London 1934.

27.   Ford Madox Ford, *Parade's End (No More Parades)*, New York 1972, 314–19.

28.   Ford, *Parade's End (Some Do Not...)*, 178. (My italics.)

12

'These hills are too green':
the English American Sylvia Plath

Tracy Brain

Sylvia Plath's position as transatlantic, as no longer entirely American but not quite English either, was of serious importance to her work. Homi Bhabha alludes to the postmodern 'contingency and ambivalence in the positioning of cultural and political identity'.[1] There is nothing new in arguing that Sylvia Plath's writing dramatises just such indeterminacy. But what I want to argue here, and what has not been said before, is that one particular site where Plath stages this drama over identity is the space between England and America.

That Sylvia Plath should preserve her Americanness mattered greatly to her family and friends. Yet Plath's speaking voice, like the language of her poetry and prose, was not hermetically sealed, and so became tainted by the linguistic and cultural bath that was England. Donning her family-pleasing voice, Plath writes in a letter to an American relative: 'I am delighted you think I have an English accent, Dotty. Everybody over here thinks I come from the Deep *South*; they think my American accent is so broad' (*L* 486).[2] This incident is representative of the predicament Plath's transatlantic national identity became for her: a predicament of between-ness, of being neither sufficiently American nor properly English. Plath institutes a twofold rhetorical strategy for dealing with what is really Dotty's polite and hurt accusation that she has betrayed her roots by losing her accent. First, Plath reinforces the charade that the accusation is a compliment. Second, and with some truth and justification, she claims that nobody can tell where she's from. An acquaintance who saw Plath during that last, difficult month of her life, writes of Plath's 'bright smile and eager American expression' (*L* 496), attempting to reassure Plath's mother of her daughter's normality. Implicit here is the idea that as long as Plath remains intrinsically American, she will be fine. To use Plath's own words, 'health' will not be 'a country far away' (*C* 162) if that country can be carried within Plath herself.

Plath's family and friends are not alone in their attempts to own Plath through sharing her nationality. Jeni Couzyn's *The Bloodaxe Book of Contemporary Women Poets* is subtitled *Eleven British Writers*, despite the fact that one of these eleven is Plath.[3] Yet if Couzyn is aware of the anomaly, she feels no need to provide a rationale for her selection and notion of what constitutes national identity. The strangeness of Plath's inclusion is not even acknowledged. Plath is either convicted of being American, as she is by Anne Stevenson in *Bitter Fame*, or unconvincingly appropriated as English, as she is by Couzyn.

Janet Malcolm has recently demonstrated with great force that biography reveals more about the biographer than her subject.[4] Certainly Malcolm's argument is evidenced by the ways critics and biographers gloss over Plath's own nationality. Stevenson, herself American-born and educated in the United States, colludes with Jane Baltzell's sense of:

> Sylvia's bumptious insensitivity to the kind of behavior the British found ridiculous. Self-conscious about any appearance of naiveté or gushiness, Jane was embarrassed when Sylvia rode up to a bobby to ask in her twangy American accent for directions to 'somewhere really picturesque and collegiate' in which to eat.[5]

Surely Stevenson and Baltzell must have behaved with similarly ostentatious Americanness when they first came to England as young women. In a similar vein, Dido Merwin is described by Stevenson as possessing 'an innate sense of belonging (something Sylvia never had)'.[6] It is not simply the illogical innuendo of criticism of Plath that jars here, or even the shock of Stevenson's complacency. Rather, it is the way this passage so breathlessly misses the point: one of the most powerful aspects of Plath's work is the way it deconstructs so compellingly any possibility of that 'innate sense of belonging' which Stevenson and Baltzell, like the many critics who ignore Plath's transatlanticism, seem to need so much to believe in.

In keeping with her status of not belonging and her neither entirely American nor purely English accent, Plath's feelings about both England and America were ambivalent. Not surprisingly, she oscillates between Anglophilia and antipathy. The idealised pastoral fantasy of a green and pleasant land is made sinister by the 'large black rooks' that 'fly over quaint red-tiled rooftops' (*L* 183). English academe is not revered but criticised as a 'mean, mealy-mouthed literary world' (*L* 317) inhabited by 'grotesque Victorian dons' (*L* 214). Likewise Plath's feelings about America vacillate. One minute she wishes to escape 'this commercial American superego' (*J* 325), the next she yearns for the luxuries that are the products of this very commercialism. Hence, she can write: 'I'll be so happy to have an American kitchen ... with orange juice and egg beater and all my lovely supplies for light cookies and cakes!' (*L* 269). Jacqueline Rose asserts that '[o]nly at one point, in 1956, does America appear unequivocally positive for Plath ... as the land that is big enough for Hughes ... and an escape from the horror of Suez.'[7] Rose typifies that reductive critical blunder of overstating the case through a tunnel vision that omits all contrary evidence ('only at one point' is America 'positive'). Here she does so in order to construct Plath as politically correct and serious – like Rose herself, above any attention to kitchen supplies. Thereby Rose misses the frequency and ambiguities of Plath's positive ideas about America.

There is a moment in *The Bell Jar* that helps explain what I mean by the term transatlanticism. Esther explains to her soon-to-be ex-boyfriend:

> I could never settle down in either the country *or* the city ... If neurotic is wanting two mutually exclusive things at one and the same time, then I'm neurotic as hell. I'll be flying back and forth between one mutually exclusive thing and another for the rest of my days (*BJ* 97–8).

Transatlantic does not just describe a hybrid *accent*. In Plath's writing, it is a refusal to chose between two places. Such a mind set is nicely represented when Plath closes a letter with the signature, '[y]our puddle-jumping daughter' (*L* 165). The transatlantic subject is ever moving between two places, admitting the possibility of mutual exclusivity, while never really accepting such a state of play, speaking always with a forked tongue.[8]

The quotation in my title, '[t]hese hills are too green and sweet to have tasted salt', is taken from Plath's poem 'Blackberrying' (1961). Robyn Marsack quotes the line in her book on Plath, and says of it: 'I think foreigners ... are struck by the way lush pastureland lies along the sea in Britain'.[9] Marsack is one of few critics to touch on the sense of foreignness in Plath's work. Yet what Marsack's discussion of the poem misses is the complex nature of a perspective that is not purely American but *trans*atlantic.

The incongruity between the sweetness of green hills and harsh saltiness of the sea would be likely to strike an American from the West Coast of America, but not one from the East. The proximity between lush greenery and salt sea on the North East coast of America is not dissimilar to such a contiguity in, say, Devon. So who is speaking in 'Blackberrying'? Somebody who is alien, or somebody who is posing as such? Certainly that dubious critical activity of equating Plath with her speakers is here shown to be futile. Plath was born and raised near a sea that was not dramatically different from an English landscape, yet writes as though she were not. Bound up in the proscription against any fixing of subjectivity or nationality is Plath's defiance of any absolute fixing of geographical place.

Occasionally Plath does invoke stereotypes of differences between England and America. For instance, she describes herself and an American friend as 'enthusiastic, demonstrative, and perhaps trusting and credulous to the point of naiveté. A strong contrast to the Englishmen, who have a kind of brittle, formal rigidity and, many of them, a calculated sophisticate pose' (L 317). Despite such moments, Plath's writing more often than not destabilises and re-ascribes such caricatured identities in surprising ways.

'Snow Blitz' (1963), a semi-autobiographical piece spoken by an amused and bewildered American woman trying to survive a cold London winter, quite explicitly constructs the English as another species. From the first sentence, it is clear that the narrator is an alien, and that the implied reader, like her, is non-English. 'In London, the day after Christmas (Boxing Day) – it began to snow: my first snow in England' (JP 125).

The implied reader is constructed as unknowing and American, in need of a definition of the very English term 'Boxing Day'. Even illness is seen as foreign. 'Flu is 'that British alternation of fever and chills for which my doctor offered no relief or cure' (JP 132). The story's humour turns on the narrator's stereotypical assumption that the English are backward in their use of technology, that they can no more cope with viruses than frozen pipes. The narrative voice sustains itself through an amused and relieved conviction of its own difference. She survives by emphasising her distance from these events, and a consequent illusion that her foreignness renders her immune to the situation. Yet contradictorily, she survives also by taking on a readily available English persona of brisk blitz-courage: '[d]ress up warm, lots of tea and bravery' (JP 133).

In 'Stone Boy with Dolphin' (1957/58), Miss Minchell, the English, 'tight-lipped', college secretary, disapproved:

> when the American girls started wearing pajamas to breakfast under their bathrobes. All British girls in the college came down fully dressed and starched ... Ample quarter pounds of butter were allotted each girl on Sunday morning to last through the week. Only gluttons bought extra butter ... and slathered it double-thick on toast while Miss Minchell dipped her dry toast with disapproval into her second cup of tea (JP 300–1).

These are familiar stereotypes. Americans are free and expressive to the point of vulgarity, materially over-privileged, greedily consumerist, and hedonistic. The English are uptight, repressed, ascetic. The narrative voice is implicated in the viewpoint of the American heroine Dodo. It is a voice that is sympathetic to America, constructing a democratic free-spiritedness in resistance to oppressive and ungenerous rules.

As Plath's own critics and biographers have ably (though usually unwittingly) demonstrated on the corpse of Plath herself, the values attributed to the poles of this binary opposition can easily be shifted. American generosity can become greed while English meanness can be seen as 'green' thrift: recycling in sympathy with the world's limited materials. Anne Stevenson's treatment of Plath in the infamous *Bitter Fame* is indicative of this shift. Here, Plath is repeatedly and disapprovingly viewed as an extravagant consumer, spurning the 'secondhand shops' and offers of furniture from friends that are a part of English life and surprising her acquaintances by wearing 'new outfits' despite her assertions of poverty.[10] This attitude is replicated by Lucas Myers, himself American, in his appendix to *Bitter Fame*. Contrasting Plath's attitude to her work with Hughes's, he writes: 'Sylvia was determined that it should be read. Ted was determined that it should exist'.[11] Myers juxtaposes what he sees as Plath's vulgar production of commodities with Hughes's almost religious excretion of works of art that possess an inherent value.

A refusal to acknowledge Plath's transatlanticism is one of many factors contributing to that pointless biographical enterprise of producing skewed verdicts on Plath's life. In addition, it has distorted interpretations of her poems. To acknowledge this transatlanticism, by contrast, makes possible new approaches to much-discussed poems such as 'Daddy'. 'Daddy' has been read as Plath's man-hating vengeance against her father and Ted Hughes,[12] or discussed in terms of her right to appropriate as literary material the experiences of Holocaust victims.[13] Yet no critic has noticed the way Plath uses 'Daddy' to explore the status of any national identity as contingent and impure – a thesis appropriate to a poem that invokes the Jews, who were persecuted for their own supposedly impure ethnicity.

In the poem, the very indeterminacy over identity that at first inhibits language becomes the key to language. Initially, the speaker:

> Never could tell where you
> Put your foot, your root,
> I never could talk to you.
> The tongue stuck in my jaw.

To unstick her tongue the speaker tells us, 'I began to talk like a Jew/I think I may well be a Jew' and finally, 'I may be a bit of a Jew' (*C* 223). In the face of no sure nationality, the sense that she possesses no native tongue, the speaker's strategy is to adopt different voices that are not entirely, if they are at all, her own.

A new approach to 'Leaving Early' is also presented if we consider it in light of Plath's transatlanticism. To make her case that the poem is about lesbianism, Janice Markey attempts to fix the gender identities of the poem's speaker, and her or his sexual partner, as female.[14] Jacqueline Rose unquestioningly assumes the speaker is male; gender is not even an issue for her.[15] This critical move of stabilising gender identities not only masks Plath's important project of questioning sexual identity itself, but also hides a concatenation between unspecified gender and ambiguous nationality. The poem's last three lines do not merely dramatise the speaker's disorientation as somebody who has woken up in an unfamiliar place after a sexual encounter with a stranger. They also enact the confusion of an American in England:

> Lady, what am I doing
> With a lung full of dust and a tongue of wood,
> Knee-deep in the cold and swamped by flowers? (*C* 146)

'Lady' is a typically American mode of address often deployed in irritation. While the expression does not establish absolutely the speaker's gender (women can of course address other women in this way), it does suggest that she or he is American. Through its mocking allusion to the English upper classes, the word 'Lady' aligns the speaker's sexual partner with Englishness. The numerous references in the poem to English things that seem strange also emphasise the speaker's status as alien, and associate the sexual partner with a derivative and pitiful 'Englishness' that is constructed by cheap objects. For instance, there is the cold that anticipates 'Snow Blitz'. There are the flowers for which England is famous but which here are disparaged as decaying and too numerous. There are the 'Coronation goblets' and the 'toby jug'. But most pressingly, the speaker's feeling of '"*unheimlich*" ... the opposite of what is familiar',[16] is experienced through language itself, through an inability to communicate in the Lady's language. Hence the 'tongue of wood'.

Such an estrangement from language becomes the central subject of 'New Year on Dartmoor' (1962). The poem can be read as the speaker's address to a young child. It describes the painful process of coming into language, of being interpellated into a symbolic order that is not your own. Yet the poem can also be read as a galling self-address through which the speaker plays out her own alienation from a discourse that appears superficially to be her own, yet is foreign. At the very least the speaker's position is one of identification with the child's isolation:

> This is newness: every little tawdry
> Obstacle glass-wrapped and peculiar,
> Glinting and clinking in a saint's falsetto. Only you
> Don't know what to make of the sudden slippiness,
> The blind, white awful, inaccessible slant.

There's no getting up it by the words you know.
No getting up by elephant or wheel or shoe (*C* 176).

I think the 'glinting', 'clinking', 'saint's falsetto' describes an American's first impression of an English accent. The 'sudden slippiness', the 'inaccessible slant' evokes social and linguistic codes that provide an illusion of familiarity, but then shift in ways that maintain the speaker's or child's position as outside: a position mimicked by the separation of 'Only you' from the sentence it begins. The 'words you know' are both American speech and baby talk: the metonymic 'elephant', 'wheel', and 'shoe' that are not merely physical means of transport, but modes of communication. In this poem, the relation between American speech and English is like that of Kristeva's pre-Oedipal semiotic to the grammatically and culturally ordered symbolic, or like that of the genotext to the syntactic phenotext.[17] In 'New Year on Dartmoor', the 'words you know' are inscribed within the established order of language: here, English. But they occupy a position that is oppressed as well as potentially subversive. It is the position of the American in England. In a surprising reversal of the hierarchy which would assume America to be powerful and England oppressed, Plath highlights the contingency of these positions: an emphasis supported by the sense of England as first, as original.

Alicia Ostriker argues that Plath's voice is 'distinctly American' because it 'represent[s] life without falsification'.[18] Playing on 'Lady Lazarus', Ostriker believes Plath 'do[es] it, technically, so it feels real'. For Ostriker, the 'brusque, business-like, and bitchy' quality of the speech of the *Ariel* poems renders them an 'American language'.[19] She cites 'Cut' (1962) as an example. Ostriker is absolutely right to identify the American vernacular that seeps into Plath's work, but the claim prevents her from recognising the moments where this voice breaks down or becomes contaminated by other languages. Ostriker's culturally and nationally absolutist view of Plath elides not just Plath's personal view of herself as hybrid, but the thematic and technical cross-breeding of her poems.

However American its expression, 'Cut' is a poem whose central activity is to complicate any possibility of a pure American identity. The poem enacts the transatlantic flux between Englishness and American-ness. The speaker gazes at her thumb, the top of which she has sliced off while cutting an onion. Using the vocabulary American school children are taught when learning about the settling of America and the American Revolution, speaking as if to an injured child, she describes the appendage:

Little pilgrim,
The Indian's axed your scalp.

Your turkey wattle
Carpet rolls

Out of a gap
A million soldiers run,
Redcoats, every one (*C* 235).

Certainly this poetic language defamiliarises the sliced and bleeding thumb, as well as the vagina leaking menstrual fluid. Yet the bodily experience, the physical split of the skin flap, comes to represent an incorporeal division of identity itself. The thumb whose outside appearance is described through images that are American is separated into pieces. What emerges from inside the American shell is alien: the Redcoats who were America's opponents during the revolution. The outside layer of familiar American history contains the British enemy within.

The 'other', that scapegoated signifier of difference and alienation, is always already within the self. Kristeva has argued that the abject is that which is 'opposed to I', and thus that which the subject attempts to exclude in order to construct her own identity. Abjection is strongest when the subject 'finds the impossible within'. Abjection is caused by that which 'disturbs identity, system, order. What does not respect borders, positions, rules. The in-between, the ambiguous, the composite.' Abjection is 'directed against a threat that seems to emanate from an exorbitant outside or inside ... It lies there, quite close, but it cannot be assimilated.'[20] For Plath, by contrast, this threat, difference itself, *can* be assimilated. In 'Cut', the bleeding gash is a 'border passable in both directions by pleasure and pain' (*C* 61). For Kristeva, '[m]enstrual blood ... stands for the danger issuing from within the identity (social or sexual); it threatens ... the identity of each sex in the face of sexual difference.'[21] In 'Cut', as in so much of Plath's work, the threat is not just to sexual difference, but also to differences of nationality – the borders not just of skin and gender, but also of country.

As is so often the case in the writing of the puddle-jumping Plath, the Redcoats aren't coming. They were there all along. The American subject is trans-Atlantic, liquescent and porous, before she has even stepped off her native soil.

NOTES

1.   Homi Bhabha, 'Postcolonial authority and postmodern guilt', in Lawrence Grossberg *et al*, eds., *Cultural Studies*, New York 1992, 59.

2.   Throughout, *L* refers to Sylvia Plath's *Letters Home*; *C* to *Collected Poems*; *JP* to *Johnny Panic and the Bible of Dreams and Other Prose Writings*; *BJ* to *The Bell Jar*; and *J* to *The Journals of Sylvia Plath*.

3.   Jeni Couzyn, ed., *The Bloodaxe Book of Contemporary Women Poets: Eleven British writers*, Newcastle-upon-Tyne 1985.

4.   Janet Malcolm, *The Silent Woman: Sylvia Plath and Ted Hughes*, New York 1994. First published in *The New Yorker*, August 23rd/30th 1993, 94–159.

5.   Anne Stevenson, *Bitter Fame: A life of Sylvia Plath*, London 1989, 64.

6.   ibid., 193.

7.   Jacqueline Rose, *The Haunting of Sylvia Plath*, London 1991, 197–8.

8.   Nicole Ward Jouve, *White Woman Speaks with Forked Tongue*, London 1991, 19.

9.   Robyn Marsack, *Sylvia Plath*, Buckingham 1992, 7.

10. Stevenson, op. cit., 181, 274, 284.

11. ibid., 314.

12. ibid., 268.

13. Rose, op. cit., and George Steiner, 'Dying is an art', in Charles Newman, ed., *The Art of Sylvia Plath: A symposium*, London 1970, 211–18.

14. Janice Markey, *A Journey into the Red Eye: The poetry of Sylvia Plath – a critique*, London 1993, 20–1.

15.   Rose, op. cit., 134.

16.   'Leaving Early' does not just suggest the uncanny as that which is unknown. The sense of the uncanny as 'the "double" ... the uncanny harbinger of death' might explain the dead roses and the 'chrysanthemums ... /In the mirror' (C 146). See Sigmund Freud, 'The Uncanny', in *The Penguin Freud Library*, Vol. 14, 341, 357.

17.   Julia Kristeva, trans. Margaret Waller, *Revolution in Poetic Language*, New York 1984, 86: '[d]esignating the genotext in a text requires pointing out the transfers of drive energy that can be detected in phonematic devices ... such as rhyme ... and melodic devices (such as intonation or rhythm)'.

18.   Alicia Ostriker, 'The Americanisation of Sylvia', in Linda W. Wagner, ed., *Critical Essays on Sylvia Plath*, Boston 1984, 99–100.

19.   ibid., 101.

20.   Julia Kristeva, *Powers of Horror: An essay on abjection*, New York 1982, 1–5.

21.   ibid., 71.

13

The dis/embodiment of culture:
the migrant in V. S. Naipaul and Bharati Mukherjee

Gail Low

This essay is a preliminary speculation on a wider project to do with migrancy and displacement – and the manner in which those experiences, and the series of expectations generated by those issues – impact upon our understanding of cultural and national identity. These sets of concerns have developed into an exploration of the manner in which the corporate national body (the body-politic) is thought through the corporeal physical body. In other words, embodiment and disembodiment, and how these metaphors structure the way we think and react to the figure of the post-colonial migrating to former imperial and metropolitan centres.

Where the dominant discourse surrounding national identity focuses on 'national culture', it has invariably read national culture as uniform culture; the national is here equated with the natural and organic body. Citizenship is thus conditioned on a unity of identity, and equality of rights is conflated with sameness. Here, full citizenship translates not only into equal status in public and political life but a unity of culture that transcends all cultural differences. Conflating equal rights with sameness denies the existence of different groups within the nation, and at times the incommensurable differences within these groups. This denial of difference effects the exclusion of some groups from public and political life: it demands that the individual suppress his or her affiliations to a cultural community that is not within the pale for him or her to be endowed with full citizenship rights. One casualty is that the migrant positioned within that overdetermined space of colonial mimicry or exoticised difference is almost always framed within a mutually exclusive rhetorical twin set of assimilation within or exclusion from the discourses of the national body. In the logic of assimilation, citizenship becomes an 'ideological yardstick for measuring the entitlement of worthy applicants to residence.'[1]

David Lloyd argues that racism is not only a cultural construct but is the 'structure of culture'. He asserts that post-Enlightenment discourses of culture produce and reproduce race as the 'constitutive negation of identity which the state represents': 'whiteness is the metaphor for the metaphorical production of the Subject as one devoid of properties rather than the natural sign of difference to which the attributes of civilization and culture are in turn attached.'[2] In Lloyd's estimation of imperial metropolitan cultures, assimilation represents a

'Catch 22' situation, for it demands deracination: 'the process of assimilation for the colonized is one which discovers within the identity which is to be formed the difference on which assimilation's very logic depends.'[3] As an invisible norm, whiteness is not a colour but an absence of colour. Whiteness is a disembodied entity. Burgin, drawing on Kristeva, pursues the ramifications of such a subject:

> [t]o speak of the colour of skin is to speak of a body. 'People of colour' are embodied people. To have no colour is to have no body. The body denied here however, is a very particular body, it is the abject body: the body that defecates, vomits and bleeds; the entopic body that dies.[4]

From Fanon we have the dual movement of racism as simultaneous embodiment and disembodiment. Here colour secures the projected racial narrative history: 'I was responsible at the same time for my body, for my race, for my ancestors ... I discovered my blackness, my ethnic characteristics; and I was battered down by tom-toms, cannibalism, intellectual deficiency, fetichism [sic], racial defects, slave ships.'[5]

It is with this preoccupation with the metaphoric overlap between deracination, disembodiment, assimilation and the construction of identity that I turn to Naipaul and Mukherjee and the reception of their work. Both John Thieme and Rob Nixon employ the term 'cultural deracination'. Nixon's critique of Naipaul's post-colonial detachment is entitled 'Naipaul and Caribbean Deracination'[6] while Thieme, commenting on the contradictory dynamics of Naipaul's fiction, writes: 'like Conrad, Naipaul has been absorbed into the English literary tradition and yet continues to see himself as a displaced outsider. In his fiction deracination has been a recurrent theme.'[7] A. Sivanadan's accusation of cultural betrayal shares similar territory: 'he had so soon, so readily become acceptable to the English literati, so easily assimilable ... From the moment "they accept you, you are finished, completed; the moment they adopt you you have sold out ... you have no existence apart from them".'[8] Other hostile responses describe Naipaul as a 'smart restorer of the comforting myths of the white race', 'England's favourite 19th-century Englishman', and 'ask him why he hates the colour of his skin so much'.[9]

To date, excepting Emmanuel Nelson's, there has been no substantial study of Mukherjee, but her own interviews and critical gloss of her own work seem to contain metaphoric reverberations of assimilation and disembodiment. Mukherjee seems to react against the multi-cultural and anti-racist agenda in American cultural life which focuses on the recovery of histories and traditions as crucial to the creation of cultural identities that resist marginalisation or erasure. Here the past is not simply a matter of temporal precedence, but is retroactive and projective – it actively creates spaces that transform present reality. Mukherjee rejects this paradigm. She is not concerned with reconstituting cultural identities (she argues that this creates cultural ghettoes) and actively resists the label of diasporic Indian writer. Instead, she speaks about migration and immigration. She rejects the Canadian policy of multiculturalism (the 'cultural mosaic') as a policy of deliberate exclusions which create second-class citizens.[10] Immigration is a process of 'letting go' in order to claim the right to belong and to be heard. She argues that the move from Canada to America was a 'movement away from the aloofness of expatriation to the exuberance of immigration', and that 'by the time time I came to write *The Middleman*, I was exhilarated, my vision was more optimistic. I knew where I wanted to be. And though I was moving in degrees of acculturation, the overall authorial vision is ... consistent.'[11] To be fair to Mukherjee, she calls this process a process of mongrelisation (a term she takes from Rushdie): 'for me ... letting go of the old concept of who you are and what America is is healthy ... I'm saying that we haven't come to accommodate or to mimic, we have changed ourselves but we have also come to change you.'[12]

While being quite different kinds of writers – Naipaul insisting on his status as alien and Mukherjee affirming her identity as American – there are areas of overlap between Naipaul's work and Mukherjee (she acknowledges him as an early model for her writing which she rejects later). I shall only look at one area in this essay – the employment of the body as symbol – and mention another: the emptying-out of the first-person narrative voice. With regards to the latter, Mukherjee's first-person narratives in *Middleman* and in *Jasmine* are not filled with plenitude and security of agency, presence and identity but are turned inside out so that they only gain coherence through being the site which registers the gaze of others. Naipaul's *Enigma of Arrival* is characterised by similar distance and vulnerability.[13] The autobiographical and fictional 'I' which ruminates, describes, retreats from society, gains coherence not by purposeful activity (though it is the 'I' that writes) nor generic authority (the book is part pastoral, travel-writing, journal, documentary, autobiography and fiction and does smooth over the disjuncture between genres) but by being the site of memories, desires, interpersonal interactions and projections. The self that emerges from Naipaul's *Arrival* is a palimpsest of other narratives, histories and ways of seeing which are inscribed upon the body of the 'I'. Yet this alienated modernist 'I', as critics have attested, is also disembodied by virtue of being unanchored in present time and culture.

But to return to my first concern with the symbolic functions of the corporeal body in Mukherjee, I have to say that my reading of Mukherjee differs somewhat from the picture of exuberant immigration and assimilation that she herself has painted. Her collection of short stories, *Middleman*, and her second novel, *Wife*, explore the theme of alienation and madness in ways that paint a dystopic view of America. *Wife* is a tale of gender and cultural displacement which traps the story's heroine between worlds and times. The wife's disembodiment is the result of traditional and new familial, cultural and gender expectations of normative behaviour. The story of Dimple Basu's life is the ideal wife of marriage adverts, the reader of woman's magazines and the anxious young woman who writes a desperate letter to the agony aunt of *Eve's Beauty Basket*:

> dear Miss problem-walla ... there is just one annoying flea in my ointment. The flea is my flat chest. As I am sure you realise, this defect will adversely affect my chances of securing an ideal husband ... Therefore I'm sure you will agree it is imperative that I do something about my problem and enhance my figure to the best of my ability. Please do not, I beg you, advocate chicken soup ... exercises and massages. I have tried them already.[14]

Dimple is also the wife of the age-old story of Sita and the denial of self: 'in Dimple's dreams, she became Sita, the ideal wife of Hindu legends, who had walked through fire at her husband's request.'[15] In America, caught between different expectations laid on her by her husband and friends, and the different culture she lives in, Dimple's own sense of self and community are eroded:

> conveying New York ... her nightmares, the 'phase' (as Amit called it) she was going through – all impossible to talk about, let alone describe in English or Bengali. She would have to give up trying to write. She would give up trying to preserve old friendships. Because there was nothing to describe and nothing to preserve.

Instead what results is a repetitive fantasy of bodily immolation:

> [b]etween three and four the next morning Dimple thought of seven ways to commit suicide in Queens. The surest way, she felt, would be to borrow a can of Drano from under the kitchen sink and drink it, diluted slightly with water. She could see herself as a Before and After type of TV commercial: human face and feet and an S-trap for a body.[16]

Dimple's psychic state is manifested through her relationship with her body; her psychological changes are embodied changes (this book is full of images of entopic bodies). She wears Marsha Mookerji's clothes to become the cosmopolitan urbanite. Sipping wine, she copies Marsha's mannerisms, 'sipping delicately, keeping her glass high and her little finger extended', to be a little like the 'women in commercials'. Dimple's fragmented identity is expressed through the incongruous juxtapositions of startlingly different mythic and media images of her body – between the body and personality she desires and the body and personality that she imagines herself as. Her descent into madness is again expressed through body image and a wish for disembodiment: 'in a mirror across the room, she saw herself, a small, stiff lump, hair arranged like black bat wings against the sky blue pillow. Catch a fatal disease, she told herself. Of all fatal diseases, leukaemia was the most glamorous.'

The short story, 'A Wife's Story', treats with more detachment and ironic humour the cultural, spatial and temporal shifts described in *Wife*. Panna Bhatt's story traverses familial and national boundaries, continents, histories and technologies. It includes finishing schools, riots, uprootings, arranged marriages, a son's death, post-graduate education in America and nights watching MTV on cable television. The phases of adjustments are accelerated, as Mukherjee comments, assimilation, nostalgia, reassertion and reinvention all occur within one generation, as opposed to spanning several.[17] But, in a distinct echo of Naipaul, the freedom from the enclosed spaces of the national, cultural and familial is a form of alienation and disembodiment. Panna remarks:

> I feel light, almost free. Memories of Indian destitutes mix with the hordes of New York street people, and they float free, like astronauts inside my head. I'm making something of my life. I've left home, my husband, to get a Ph.D in special ed. I have a multiple-entry visa and a small scholarship for two years. My mother was beaten by her mother-in-law, my grandmother when she registered for French lesson at the *Alliance Française*. My grandmother, the eldest, was illiterate.[18]

In an echo of the Lacanian metaphor, the story ends with her disembodiment in the bathroom mirror. Catching sight of the image of her body in that other space, Panna imagines herself as free, afloat and 'watching somebody else'.

In many ways this story echoes Naipaul's earlier short story, 'One out of Many', where the servant-character also looks in the mirror and discovers an image of himself after sexual relations with a black cleaner. Sexual relations, and his gradual familiarity with American customs and language signal both a growing rift with his culture and with his benevolent patron, and a coming into his own: '[n]ow I found that, without wishing it, I was ceasing to see myself as part of my employer's presence and beginning at the same time to see him as

116

an outsider might see him'.[19] Yet instead of seeing this development as positive, the tale ends bleakly with his marriage to the black cleaner, symbol of all he finds ritually polluting. The freedom gained is a dubious sort of freedom and turns out instead to be a disembodiment and an alienation:

> I was once part of the flow, never thinking of myself as a presence. I looked in the mirror and decided to be free. All that my freedom has brought me is the knowledge that I have a face and a body, that I must feed this body and clothe this body for a certain number of years. Then it will be over.[20]

Naipaul's fiction returns obsessively to the themes of exile and homelessness; his portrait of the post-colonial is one of an impresario or mimic man who has no real culture or authentic identity but is forever doomed to hollowness and repetition. All of these themes can be figured as a disembodiment and an alienation. Yet what is also puzzling in Naipaul is an extreme anxiety about the body and embodiment. The Santosh character's downfall in *In a Free State* represents entrapment by the body of the *hubshi*, a revenge of the body as pollutant. The idea of the body as pollutant is borne out by the images of bodily smells, dirt, excrement, decay and corruption that India is equated with in *An Area of Darkness*. (Similar instances of this indictment of the body and its material functions occur in Mukherjee's interview with Michael Connell and in her first novel, *The Tiger's Daughter*.)[21] Critics have attributed these images to a Brahmanical hypersensitivity to pollution, but this preoccupation with the body (expressed in part as a desire to rid oneself of the body) might also be indicative of a desire to be aloof, free from, to be disembodied, to transcend bodily demands and all they represent. For example, in *The Enigma of Arrival*, Naipaul uses the body symbolically to address the vulnerability of the formerly colonised: he links the state of the body (its vulnerability) to colonial relations, and later, to power relations. For example, the narrator's arrival in England is marked by a 'nervousness in a new place, that rawness of response', the strangeness was 'like the tearing at an old scab'.[22] Elsewhere, he talks about having the nerves of being a stranger in England: 'I had taken to England all the rawness of my colonial's nerves, and those nerves had more or less remained, nerves which in the beginning were in good part also the nerves of youth and inexperience, physical and sexual inadequacy, and of undeveloped talent.'[23] The allusion to the racial body is not direct but by inference. The rawness of nerves that the young writer possesses can be gleaned from his thoughts on the two black men he meets on the boat:

[t]he muscular weight-lifting Trinidad Negro in tight, buttoned-up sports
jacket in Puerto-Rico on the way to Harlem; the other black man on the
S S Columbia handling himself carefully, returning to the life in Germany
he preferred to his life in the US – these men in whom (unwillingly since I
was Indian and Hindu, full of the tragedy and glory of India) I saw aspects
of my self, echoes of my own journey and the yearning at the back of that
journey, these men had been isolated in 1950, vulnerable, their nerves raw
... the rawness of nerves among black people had become like a communal
festering.[24]

Other instances of the body's return – a reminder of racial embodiment and
vulnerability – is expressed by the recurring dream of the exploding head.

Yet disembodiment in Naipaul also stems from a desire to be aloof, to
withdraw into the shell of the observing I: 'not an observer merely, a man
removed; but a man played on, worked on by many things.' The narrator talks
of looking down at the landscape from the great height of the aeroplane as an
act that brought Trinidad home to him: 'a landscape of clear pattern and
contours, absorbing all the roadside messiness, a pattern of dark green and dark
brown, like camouflage, like a landscape in a book, like a landscape of a real
country.'[25] Aloofness and detachment seem also to be part of Mukherjee's
project in so far as her first-person narratives operate as disembodied voices:
either her characters' subjection to racism in America renders them estranged,
or the attempt to transcend their country of origin manifests itself as a flight
from the body, a certain distancing from the body politic. In an article for the
New York Times, she refers to her 'chameleon-skinned' ability to move across
social and ethnic divides without difficulty. The metaphor is problematic because
if it signals a recognition of cultural differences, it also signals a disavowal of
those differences.

Teaching *Middleman* has always been difficult precisely because of the
apparent ease of inhabitation of different voices and cultural communities – but
is this to do more with expectations generated with what she as an 'Indian'
writer represents? Are Thieme and Nixon right to talk about deracination in
relation to Naipaul? What is Naipaul (un)consciously implying when he calls
attention to the body in the manner that he does? What kinds of expectations are
generated from these metaphors that resort to the body and the embodiment of
culture? Conversely, Naipaul's detachment has been elsewhere praised as a form
of transcendence. For some critics, it is his role as the disinterested and aloof
observer that has made him a citizen of the world despite his seeming
unbelonging. Irving Howe elevates his deracination in a diametrically opposed

sense to Thieme and Nixon by declaring that Naipaul's 'deracination ... enables a steely perspective, the scaped honesty of the margin ... cool precision.'[26]

Two sides to disembodiment – disembodiment as alienation/assimilation on the one hand, and disembodiment as transcendence on the other – as a universality that turns on precisely the same problems as outlined by Lloyd and Burgin. Two sides of the same problematic coin – two sides of the same trap? The difficulty of reading Naipaul and Mukherjee lies in the fact that a new language is perhaps needed that preserves the complexity and ambivalence of the political agenda and its affiliative and filiative ties. Such a language will also need to address the interface between individual and social space and between culture as ancestry and cultural as communal and material present.[27]

NOTES

1. Phil Cole, 'The Idea of Citizenship in a Multicultural Community', a paper read at the Staffordshire University Research Forum; for a critique of universal citizenship, see Iris Marion Young, *Throwing Like a Girl*, Bloomingdale 1990, chapters 6 and 7.

2. David Lloyd, 'Race Under Representation', *Oxford Literary Review*, 13:1/2 (1991), 87, 77.

3. ibid., 85.

4. Victor Burgin, 'Paranoic Space', *New Formations*, 12 (1990), 69.

5. Frantz Fanon, *Black Skins, White Masks*, Oxford 1967.

6. Rob Nixon, *London Calling: V. S. Naipaul, postcolonial mandarin*, New York 1992, 19.

7. John Thieme, *The Web of Tradition: Uses of allusion in V. S. Naipaul's fiction*, London 1987, 13.

8. A. Sivanadan, 'The Enigma of the Colonised: Reflections on Naipaul's *Arrival*', *Race and Class*, 32:1 (1990), 33.

9. Quoted in Nixon, op. cit., 4.

10. Bharati Mukherjee, 'When in America', *Bazaar*, 13 (1990), 8–9.

11. Bharati Mukherjee, *Darkness*, New York 1992.

12. Mukherjee, 'When in America', 9.

13. V. S. Naipaul, *The Enigma of Arrival*, Harmondsworth 1987.

14. Bharati Mukherjee, *Wife*, New York 1975, 10.

15. ibid., 6.

16. ibid., 102.

17. Mukherjee, 'When in America', 9.

18. Bharati Mukherjee, *Middleman and Other Stories*, London 1990, 28–9.

19. V. S. Naipaul, *In a Free State*, Harmondsworth 1973, 37.

20. ibid., 57–8.

21. Michael Connell, 'An Interview with Bharati Mukherjee', *The Iowa Review*, 20:3 (1990), 7–32.

22. Naipaul, *The Enigma of Arrival*, 13.

23. ibid., 95.

24. ibid., 145.

25. ibid., 97.

26. Quoted in Nixon, op. cit., 37.

27. Though I am not sure that this is always preserved by the current glib exhaltation of textual and cultural hybridity and migrancy.

14

Fields for the faction fights: poetry, icons, nationalisms

Tom Herron

In this essay I consider the field as both a shared and contested cultural and political icon in Irish nationalist and Northern Irish loyalist identities.[1] I suggest that the field should be seen as part of a system of iconic representations that are constantly replicated as powerful signifiers and metaphors of national and cultural identity: others might be the Tricolour, the Red Hand of Ulster, images of William III at the Battle of the Boyne, the hunger-striker, the Orange, the Green, and so on. My interest here is on how the field operates in some contemporary Irish poetry, paying particular attention to Ciaran Carson's poem 'Campaign', a text that establishes productive play around the term 'field'.

The field has long been used as a symbol of the essential unity of the Irish nation. In the famous ballad 'Four Green Fields', the old woman's grief is voiced within the context of usurpation; she insists on the integrity of the four green fields which are simultaneously one green field (as unity is broken by the loss of one of its constituent parts). The song is a parable of the partition of Ireland in 1920, but its sentiments extend back to the seventeenth-century plantations of Ulster by English and Scottish settlers. The final verse goes as follows:

'What did I have?' said the fine old woman.
'What did I have?' the fine old woman did say.
'I had four green fields,
each one was a jewel.
But strangers came
and tried to take one from me.
I had fine strong sons
who fought to save my jewel.
They fought and died
and that was my grief', said she.

It is a particularly effective voicing of the perceived loss of organic unity by the colonised subject, within colonised space. That the woman is quite clearly a Mother Ireland figure re-establishes the well-worn associations between Ireland and the female body; a connection which is now supplemented by the image of the field, which is itself often imagined in feminine terms. The main features I want to emphasise about the song are its utilisation of the field as a symbol for national and natural unity, and its introduction of the field as a site of struggle, and (temporary) defeat. We can see how the field is here mobilised within nationalist mythology to present an image of the actual condition of Ireland (which is debased) and its visionary, imagined condition (which is utopian).

Clare O'Halloran has suggested that the sense of loss of the 'fourth green field' has profoundly influenced Southern Irish nationalist perceptions of the North and, indeed, of the island as a whole. On the first page of *Partition and the Limits of Irish Nationalism*, she refers to Oliver MacDonagh's assertion that 'in one sense the Irish problem has persisted because of the power of geographical images over men's minds'[2] and she states that representations of Ireland as a unified whole, and of the fourth green field as the lost component, 'had a particular importance in expressing the irredentist core of the ideology [of nationalism]. In spite of partition the nationalist map image was of the whole island as a distinct geographical entity, bounded by the sea and with no internal divisions.'[3] Later, she cites a fascinating range of anti-partitionist statements concerned both with the loss of the 'fourth green field' (that is, the six partitioned counties of the province of Ulster), but also with that lost territory's essential Irishness. Eamonn de Valera's radio broadcast to the American people on Abraham Lincoln's birthday (12th February 1933) epitomises such views of the North:

[t]he area that Ireland has lost contains many of the holiest and most famous places. There is Armagh, the See of St Patrick; Downpatrick, his burial place, where lies also the body of Brian who drove out the Danish; Bangor, the site of one of Ireland's ancient schools; Derry of St Columcille; Tyrone of the O'Neills' MacArt's Fort, where Wolfe Tone swore to work for Irish freedom; Belfast, the birthplace of the Irish Republican movement.[4]

It is useful to remember that de Valera's vision of Ireland was based strongly on the integrity offered by the field and its metonymies:

[t]he Ireland that we dreamed of would be the home of a people who valued material wealth only as the basis of right living, of a people who were satisfied with frugal comfort and devoted their leisure to the things of the spirit – a land whose countryside would be bright with cosy homesteads, whose fields and villages would be joyous with the sounds of industry, with the romping of sturdy children, the contests of athletic youths and the

laughter of comely maidens, whose firesides would be forums for the wisdom of serene old age.[5]

The field is not only a symbol for nationalists and republicans of the essential wholeness of the island, but it is also a central icon with Northern Irish protestant and unionist ritual and identity. In a very literal sense it is the *alpha* and the *omega* of the annual marches throughout Ulster that begin and terminate in a gathering-place that is always referred to, not merely as 'a field' but as 'the field'. Here, the field represents order, transformation of a previously marginal terrain, and the continuing hold upon a threatened territory and political entity. The field and the parades re-establish links back to the origins of unionist culture in the north of Ireland, and are consequently an extremely potent symbol for that culture. The field on these important occasions connects the participants of the parades to the Battle of the Boyne (1690) at which the Catholic King James II's armies were defeated by those of William III of Orange. The field also, by implication, recalls the Battle of the Somme in 1916, a crucial moment within Ulster's heritage: it is worth recalling that the battle actually began on the anniversary of William III's victory, and that massive numbers of Ulster soldiers died in the cause of King, country, and the Union.[6] Indeed, the field (and the parade to and from it) is a forum which simultaneously allows a ritual re-enactment of those moments of supreme importance within Northern Irish unionist and protestant culture and history, while at the same time being a stage on which contemporary political rhetoric plays a major part.

In both traditions, the field (and its metonymies, such as the Green, the site of battle, the privileged place, the origin) functions as a homeotopia, an exclusive space belonging to one side or the other, protected by walls, barriers and demarcatory practices such as ritual marches and gatherings. The field provides a glimpse of originary purity and of utopian possibilities for an imagined future society. Although I may be simplifying the preferred political and cultural outcomes of both strands of nationalism in Ireland and/or Northern Ireland, I would argue strongly that such homeotopism survives (indeed, thrives) in present-day political discourse and action. Think of the iconic images utilised by advocates of physical force in the North, and one soon realises how central the idea of territorial morphology and exclusivism remains in imagining one's nation or territory.[7] The field also seems to me to be an apposite illustration of logocentrism: the field is the centre, it is a protected inner space, surrounded by, and threatened by the other, the outside, the out-of-field. I want to propose the field as a grounding metaphor for contemporary notions of territorial and national essence, and that it is a metaphor that is employed to underpin present-day political ideologies and strategies.

Northern Irish poetry has long been aware of the importance of the field, representing as it does one more facet of that poetry's interminable obsession with land and territory. Hewitt, Kavanagh, Heaney, and Montague all locate micro-dramas of national consequence in connection with fields, and all consider the field as in some ways exemplifying the state of the nation, if not some universal condition. While all these poets (in poems such as 'The Rough Field',[8] 'The Other Side',[9] 'From the Canton of Expectation',[10] 'The Great Hunger',[11] 'Cultra Manor: The Ulster Folk Museum'[12]) present the field as a conflictual site in which submerged narratives are inscribed within the land, and reinscribed within writing, what is notable is the lack of any attention to the metaphorical valences of the field itself. Ciaran Carson's 'Campaign', on the other hand, is a poem that enacts a very potent critique of the field as an exclusive, indeed, a carceral icon. I propose a reading of the poem that foregrounds the text's disruptive strategies: in particular, its critique of the mythic unity of the field, its representation of an urban field as a palimpsest for a history of conflict, and its attention to the links between violence and unitary notions of territory and power.

Campaign

They had questioned him for hours. Who exactly was he?
    And when
He told them, they questioned him again. When they
    accepted who he was, as
Someone not involved, they pulled out his fingernails. Then
They took him to a waste-ground somewhere near the
    Horseshoe Bend, and told him
What he was. They shot him nine times.

A dark umbilicus of smoke was rising from a heap of burning
    tyres.
The bad smell he smelt was the smell of himself. Broken glass
    and knotted Durex.
The knuckles of a face in a nylon stocking. I used to see him in
    the Gladstone Bar,
Drawing pints for strangers, his almost-perfect fingers flecked
with scum.[13]

I will begin my discussion of 'Campaign' by concentrating on the relationships between the violence and the space(s) of the poem. There are two locations: the

Gladstone Bar (on the Falls Road in Belfast) and the waste-ground, near the Horseshoe Bend (the text's primary scene, and the one I am interested in here and now). The violence is clearly sectarian: the identities of the protagonists are unstated; the identity of the victim is unknown to the attackers; the *coups de grâce* are administered once it is clear that he is someone 'not involved'. It may be difficult to assimilate this picture of violence to anything other than barbarity and/or mindlessness and/or madness, but the significance of the title infiltrates and ironises each of the actions catalogued by the poem. The violence perpetrated against the victim is carried out within the motivational and ideological framework of the 'campaign', a term associated primarily with republican terrorist or guerrilla groups to indicate a tenacious adherence to a principled strategy, but one also used to describe the strategy of sectarian violence of loyalist terror squads in the early to mid-1970s.[14] This joint usage opens the poems out to both sides of the sectarian and political struggle. The discrepancy between the term 'campaign' and the sort of action perpetrated in the furtherance of that campaign is akin to the language games of the Gulf War, most notably the chasm between the term and the actuality of 'surgical air strikes'. However, the poem goes further than suggesting that sectarian attacks are simply a form of slippage from a principled form of conflict; rather, such attacks are seen as central to the political campaigns waged by all paramilitary factions in the Northern Irish conflict. Sectarian attack is a political weapon, used for specific strategic purposes – it is not necessarily a symptom of deranged minds. Sectarian attacks are as much part of the arsenal of paramilitaries as the bomb, or the assassination or murder of a British soldier or politician.

So, in order to link up the poem with 'the field', I will look closely at the poem's title. As a noun, 'campaign' can be described as 'a connected series of military operations that forms a distinct phase of a war or takes place in a particular geographical area', 'military life in the field', and as 'a connected series of operations designed to bring about a particular result'.[15] The word itself derives from 'campus', the Latin for 'field'. Carson's poem is very much aware of the contradictions implicit in the term 'campaign', both in its strategic and spatial dimensions. What the poem avoids is any suggestion that the current state of affairs (exemplified by the poem's horrific event) is a fall away from Edenic purity, but that the dystopic, detrital space of the waste-ground (the urban field) in which even the boundaries between human and non-human are dissolved is, in fact, the underside of those mythological spaces of both loyalism and nationalism. In other words, those exclusive notions of nation and identity that I suggested were imagined in terms of the field, and which find expression in the military and political campaign. Just as the waste-ground testifies to the dissolution of material objects, it poses searching questions of a political strategy that can lead to human objectification and dissolution of a waste-tip.

Several important questions remain. If I am asserting the importance of icons within contemporary nationalisms, how in fact do they operate in a material way? Do they really inform present action and consciousness? Perhaps a more productive way of thinking such icons is through an ideological model, so that icons are seen as constructed *and* constructive. This would involve uncovering a history of representation of the icon in order to show how a particular icon, at a particular time has been mobilised for particular purposes by a particular group. This is something that has already been undertaken in relation to such figures as Cuchulain, the hunger-striker, and William III. I hope that this essay will encourage similar attention being paid to the field as another significant element of Irish iconographies. Such a call has, in fact, been made before. In John Hewitt's poem 'Cultra Manor', the speaker recalls a visit to the Ulster Folk Museum. After 'looking at the enlarged photographs/of obsolete rural crafts' and folksy artefacts, his 'friend John' suggests that:

What they need now, somewhere about here,
is a field for the faction fights.[16]

Acknowledgements

Ciaran Carson: extract from *The Irish For No* (1988) reprinted by kind permission of Gallery Press.
John Hewitt: extract from *The Collected Poems of John Hewitt* (1991) reprinted by kind permission of Blackstaff Press.

NOTES

1.   I have to acknowledge my debt to Eamonn Hughes's essay, 'Northern Ireland: Border country', out of which the germ for this essay grew. See the introductory essay in Eamonn Hughes, ed., *Culture and Politics in Northern Ireland: 1960-1990*, Milton Keynes 1991.

2.   Quoted in Clare O'Halloran, *Partition and the Limits of Irish Nationalism*, Dublin 1987, 1.

3.   ibid.

4. ibid., 26.

5. Eamonn de Valera, ed. Maurice Moynihan, *Speeches and Statements by Eamonn de Valera: 1917–73*, Dublin and New York 1980, 466. It is no accident that later in the broadcast de Valera quotes Thomas Davis's 'Foreign Travel' (*The Nation*, 17th August 1844) in which an ideal Ireland is again founded upon 'fields glorious with peaceful abundance'. Quoted in Seamus Deane, ed., *The Field Day Anthology of Irish Writing*, Derry 1991, Vol. III, 748.

6. It is crucially important to remember that thousands of Southern Irish soldiers also died during the Great War.

7. The most visible illustrations of the importance of territorial and national morphologies within nationalist and loyalist identities are to be found in the political murals of Derry and Belfast. See Belinda Loftus, *Mirrors: William III and Mother Ireland*, Dundrum, Co. Down 1990; Bill Rolston, *Drawing Support: Murals in the North of Ireland*, Belfast 1992; and Rolston's *Politics and Painting: Murals and conflict in Northern Ireland*, London and Toronto 1991.

8. John Montague, *The Rough Field*, Belfast 1972.

9. Seamus Heaney, *Wintering Out*, London 1972, 34.

10. Seamus Heaney, *The Haw Lantern*, London 1987, 46.

11. Patrick Kavanagh, *The Complete Poems*, Newbridge 1972, 79.

12. John Hewitt, ed. Frank Ormsby, *The Collected Poems of John Hewitt*, Belfast 1991, 187.

13. Ciaran Carson, *The Irish For No*, Newcastle-upon-Tyne 1988, 36.

14. See Sarah Nelson, *Ulster's Uncertain Defenders: Protestant political, paramilitary and community groups and the Northern Irish conflict*, Belfast 1984.

15. *The Longman Dictionary of the English Language*, Harlow 1984.

16.   John Hewitt, op. cit., 187.

15

The Sleeping Beauty complex:
maps as text in the construction of national identity

Peter Vujakovic

The role of cartographic representations as objective 'mirrors of reality' is being questioned. Rather, they are beginning to be regarded as rhetorical texts, grounded in the values and meanings of a particular society. As texts, they propagate an argument about the world from a specific standpoint. National atlases are a particular case in point. They can be regarded as complex narrative structures, intricately weaving a story of national identity through a combination of words and images.

This essay focuses on the recently-published *Concise Atlas of the Republic of Croatia*.[1] The atlas promotes a particular view of the newly (re)created nation state of Croatia and its relationships within the political architecture of the new Europe. The version of Croatian nationhood traced in this atlas provides a classic illustration of a type of national narrative which has been dubbed the 'Sleeping Beauty complex', of which more below.[2] The *Atlas of the Republic of Croatia* provides an insight into the role of cartographic representation in the construction of national identity. The break-up of Yugoslavia during the 1990s resulted in the creation of a number of new states within the Balkan region. These states are all in the process of defining or re-defining their position as nation states within the new political structure of post-communist Europe.

Maps are an important means of describing and defining spatial concepts (for example, territorial limits, political boundaries). However, since the status of cartographic representations as factual and objective reflections of reality is being increasingly undermined, maps may now be regarded as a form of 'text', a cultural artifact which communicates the values of a particular society or individual. A critical reading of these texts seeks to unearth the hidden agendas present within cartography and the social practices and power that maps both reflect and employ.[3]

Adapting Foucault's ideas on 'the omnipresence of power in all knowledge', the historian of cartography J. B. Harley distinguishes two types of power in cartography. First, 'external power', which is exerted *on* cartography and exercised *with* cartography by the state or other authoring body. Secondly, the 'internal power', which refers to the cartographic process itself, through which regularity is imposed on the complexities of the phenomenal environment, producing a ordered image of 'reality'. All maps can be regarded as 'propagandist' in the widest sense of the word. In this context, national atlases can be seen as important ideological devices. They form a narrative, telling the story of a nation and locating the national identity in both space and time. They have a dual role in inculcating feelings of national pride and unity at home and acting as 'ambassadors' abroad.

The disintegration of Yugoslavia during the early 1990s has resulted in a number of new unitary states, each of which is now in the process of establishing and projecting its own distinctive national identity. This generally involves the (re)discovery and celebration of national histories and the assumption of the symbolic trappings of statehood. This process is crucial in a number of ways. Most importantly, it replaces the void left by the myth of a unified federal Yugoslavia with new nationalist mythologies which justify a place amongst the world's nations and create a foil to the expansionist territorial ambitions of neighbouring nation states. Maps as expressions of national territory can be critical in this process, not simply in defining the territorial space of the state, but as symbols of the link between people and place. Anderson notes the importance of the map-as-logo, a potent emblem which is instantly recognisable and can be infinitely reproduced.[4] The distinctive 'boomerang' shape of Croatia provides such an emblem. It is shown in gold on blue on the cover of the atlas, mimicking the state stars of the European Union flag.

The Atlas of Croatia opens with the following words: '[i]n 1992 the Republic of Croatia became an internationally recognised state and a member of the United Nations Organisation. Centuries-long aspiration of the Croatian people became a reality on the political map of both Europe and the World.'[5] This English language edition is primarily aimed at an international audience and at Croats in diaspora. The editor, Mladen Klemencic, claims that one of the duties of Croatia, as a new member of the world community, is to enter into the international exchange of information; to provide 'facts about the young European state and country called Croatia.'[6] The English language atlas was based partly on a Croatian language version, the *Zemljopisni atlas Republike Hrvatske (Geographical Atlas of the Republic of Croatia)* published in 1992. This consisted mainly of topographic maps and some thematic maps. The sections dealing with the history of Croatia were compiled specially for the English language edition.

The ultimate goal of nationalism is the establishment of the nation state. Croatia has achieved this end and is now in the process of consolidating its claims to statehood and territorial control. Maps have played a crucial role in national determination in the Balkans throughout this century, and the continued importance of cartographic representations is clearly understood by the Croatians. Issuing an atlas is a means of asserting and authenticating the historical links between the people and the land. Nationhood is defined by evidence of *cultural continuity* and the struggle of a *united people* to defend their territory.

The atlas creates visual representation of a historical-national space. The map of 'Land boundaries and regions' is particularly important, in that it serves to legitimise the present territory of Croatia by reference to the historical stability of its boundaries; for example, most of the Croat-Slovene border dates from the tenth to the sixteenth centuries. While more recent changes (since 1945) have frequently involved annexation of land to other republics of the former Yugoslavia, so, by implication, these are really part of the Croat nation. Hence, the loss of part of Srijem (in the eastern Croatian province of Slavonia) to Serbia in 1945 is described as an 'amputation'. This sanguinary organic analogy is graphically depicted using bright red for the recent boundaries, compared with the conservative blue and green of the older boundaries. The symbolic, metaphorical use of colour has always played a very important part in persuasive cartography – for example, the hearty rose-pink of British Empire maps.

Croatian history is extremely complex, the result of its position in a region which straddles a major cultural and political fault line. Under the rule of Rome rather than Byzantium, and later as part of the Austro-Hungarian Empire, Croatia has identified with the Catholic west rather than the Orthodox east. This association with 'the western cultural sphere' is continually emphasised throughout the atlas. Modern Croatia wishes to see itself accepted into the western European political and economic fold.

The version of Croatian history outlined in the atlas can be seen as an example of the national narrative type mentioned above, the 'Sleeping Beauty complex': this is a nationalist myth based on a 'golden age of heroes' followed by period of decline, from which the nation awakes to reclaim its past.[7] The atlas provides a sequence of historical maps which relate such a narrative.[8] The zenith of Croatia's cultural, political and military history is identified with the kingdom which ruled over much of the present territory of Croatia and Bosnia from the tenth to the twelfth centuries. Enforced union with Hungary in 1102, and later incorporation within the Hapsburg Empire, is presented as an era of heroic struggle to maintain national sovereignty. At the same time, Croatia preserved its martial pride as the *antemurale Christianitatis* (bulwark of Christendom) against Turkish incursions into western Europe. A short-lived period of national resurgence as an independent state in 1918 took Croatia into union with Serbia and Slovenia (later the Kingdom of Yugoslavia). This is characterised as the beginning of a further period of Croatian national decline, followed by the establishment of the Nazi-puppet state of the Croat *Ustasha* movement during the Second World War, and finally, the incorporation of

Croatia within socialist Yugoslavia under 'the hegemony of centralistic Belgrade'.[9] Only after the break-up of Yugoslavia do Croats achieve their centuries-long dream of building a national and democratic state. The metaphor of 'sleep-and-awakening' is clearly evident in this rendering of history.

The 'wounds' of earlier territorial losses remain fresh and form part of the continuing history of the nation. The map of 'Administrative-territorial Divisions' reflects the reality of the Croat-Serb conflict. While no direct mention is made of the self-proclaimed 'Republic of Serbian Krijina' (within Croatia) on this map, its *de facto* existence is testified to by the designation of two districts with 'a special self-governing status'. These areas have autonomous status and fall within the present United Nations Protection Force (UNPROFOR) zones. These protected areas also extend beyond the 'special districts' to cover the so-called 'pink areas', under Serb control (including parts of Slavonia in eastern Croatia). The protection of these Serb areas has been seen by some Croats as United Nations collusion in consolidating Serb territorial gains. The map clearly seeks to contain Serb control to those 'municipalities' with overall Serb majorities.

The Croat-Serb conflict also plays an important symbolic role in the atlas. It reinforces the 'myth' of Croatia as part of the civilised west, the Europe of plurality, culture and democracy. The Serbs form a symbolic 'other', an alien, barbaric influence against which patriotic sentiment of 'the entire nation' is mobilised. Maps and statistical tables bear 'witness to a (Greater) Serbian barbarian destruction', involving loss of life and the devastation of the cultural and natural heritage of Croatia.[10] The 'Turks' are also used to create a significant 'other' in this writing of history, to place Croatia firmly within the sphere of western culture. The atlas also includes topographic and thematic maps of Bosnia and Hercegovina. This is justified on the grounds of 'geographical, historical and geopolitical interrelation and ... [the] ... spatial distribution of Croatian people [in Bosnia-Hercegovina] as well as the joint war reality.'[11] While Bosnian Croats fought alongside Bosnian Muslim forces this statement may have appeared reasonable; however, since the Croats have turned their backs on their one-time allies and have emulated the brutality of Serb actions in the Republic, the inclusion of these maps takes on a more sinister complexion. Critics of the Croatian President, Franjo Tudjman, believe that he has always aimed to extend control into Bosnia-Hercegovina, with the intention of creating a 'Greater Croatia'. In 1992 Croatia was threatened with sanctions if it did not withdraw troops from Bosnia, where it was supporting the self-styled 'Croatian Union of Herceg-Bosnia'.[12]

It is also interesting to note that in 1992 the 'Bosnian Croats' renamed the Hercegovinian town of Duvno, 'Tomislavgrad', after the tenth century Croatian

King Tomislav, whose coronation place Duvno was.[13] This is another example of the importance of place and people in national mythology. It comes, therefore, as no surprise to find that 'Duvno' (within Bosnia-Hercegovina territory) is also labelled as 'Tomislavgrad' in a Croatian atlas.[14]

The close association between Croatia and the territory of Bosnia-Hercegovina also is presented in a range of linguistic and historical maps. A map showing 'Croats in neighbouring states' highlights the present concentration of Croats in Bosnia-Hercegovina, especially the Croat-dominated region of western Hercegovina. The historic links between the two republics are emphasised, especially the fact that Bosnia only surfaces as an independent political entity following Croatia's defeat at the hand of Hungary in 1097. During the earlier 'golden age' of Croatian power, much of Bosnia, often as far east as the Drina River border with Serbia, fell under the control of the 'Kingdom of Croatia'. According to this version of history all Bosnians are essentially Croats – '[d]eep changes in the Croatian ethnic territory appeared as a consequence of Turkish incursions'.[15] Hence, in this narrative, the Bosnian Muslims are simply the result of the forced 'Islamisation' of a Croat population.

Language maps are also used to lend support to this view of a wider Croatian national homeland. The use of language as a surrogate for national identity has important precursors in the Balkans. Language maps played a crucial role in solving territorial questions following the break-up of the German and Austro-Hungarian Empires at the end of the First World War. The new boundaries of Central Europe and the Balkans were founded on the principle of national self-determination. Lacking other information, national groups were often defined on the basis of language area maps which were believed to equate with nationality or ethnicity. For example, H. R. Wilkinson's 1951 study, *Maps and Politics*, describes how Jovan Cvijic, Head of Geography at Belgrade University, produced language maps which legitimised Serbian claims to Macedonia. Although it was commonly accepted, at the turn of the century, that the peoples of Macedonia were mainly of Bulgarian nationality, Cvijic was able to develop a concept of a separate group termed 'Macedo-Slavs'. Serbia, which had gained control of northern Macedonia following Bulgaria's defeat in the second Balkan War (1913), was able to extend its control based on Allied acceptance of Cvijic's maps.

Over ten percent of the thematic maps in the Croatian atlas are dedicated to showing the distribution of three 'Croatian' dialect groups within Croatia and Bosnia-Hercegovina. The maps shows Croatian dialects extending over the whole of both republics. The fact that the Stokavian dialect group (the most geographically extensive) is also spoken by Serbs is not mentioned. The detailed sub-division of the dialect groups is extremely complex and creates an illusion of a Croatian language homeland within the two republics. The issue of dialect is complex. Ivo Banac summarises the problem that the Croats face in using dialect as an basis for national identity: '[t]he unique Croatian dialectal situation, that is the use of three dialects ... could not be reconciled with the romantic belief that language was the most profound expression of national spirit. Obviously one nation could not have three spirits, nor could one dialect be shared by two nationalities.'[16]

The display of 'symbols of state' (for example, the state flag or coat of arms) also forms an important element in most national atlases. While these are not necessarily cartographic in form, they constitute an important factor in defining the geopolitical 'reality' which the state wishes to create. For example, the incorporation of these symbols within the margins and legends of maps creates a symbolic assertion of sovereignty over territory.[17] Many national symbols or 'icons' are directly geographical in their symbolic reference. An obvious case is the symbolism inherent in the stars and stripes of the flag of the United States of America. The present flag, based on an 1818 Act of Congress, consists of 13 stripes, representing the original British colonies which rebelled and formed the union, and 50 stars, representing the present total of States within the Union. The 1818 Act specified that a new star must be added to the blue field whenever another State formally enters the Union.[18] Former colonial connections or present administrative arrangements are also displayed on many national flags. The British Union Flag, for example, forms an element in numerous flags of former colonies (for example, New Zealand, Australia, Fiji) and territory administered by Britain (for example, the Virgin Islands).

The Croatian symbols of state provide a focus for patriotic pride and national unity. A section of the atlas is given over to their description. The national flag consists of horizontal bands of red, white and blue (of equal width) on which has been superimposed the Croatian coat of arms. The flag is an adaptation of the flag of the 'Kingdom of Croatia, Slavonia and Dalmatia' sanctioned by agreement with Hungary in 1868 and provides further evidence of the historical continuity of the Croatian national identity. The colours are based on the coats of arms of the three provinces; the red and silver of Croatia, the blue and silver of Slavonia and the blue of Dalmatia. Hence, the flag graphically unites the historical-geographical entities which make up the modern state of Croatia. The atlas also attempts to reinforce Croatian links with western democratic and libertarian views by verbal reference to tricolour flags as popular symbols of liberty.[19] The Croatian red and silver chequered coat of arms takes pride of place in the centre of the flag. As a whole the flag serves a similar iconic purpose to other flags with strong geographical metaphors of national unity.

However, these symbols may also serve to antagonise others, particularly the Serbs, within the population of Croatia.[20] Misha Glenny claims that Franjo Tudjman deliberately 'showered Croatia with symbols and imagery of Croatia's "glorious past"', as part of his policy aimed at alienating the Serbs: '[s]uddenly their world was being turned upside down by men wearing the same heraldry worn by the fascist *Ustashas*'.[21] Hence, the use and reuse of the medieval heraldry of Croatia provides a link to both a glorious and inglorious past.

As a discourse created and received by human agents, maps represent the world through a veil of ideology, are fraught with internal tensions, provide classic examples of power-knowledge, and are always caught up in wider political concerns.[22] *The Atlas of Croatia* clearly represents more than a depiction of bare geographic and historic fact. It provides an insight into *one* version of the values and dreams of a nation. The rhetorical position outlined in the atlas connects with the wider discourse concerning national identity in the Balkans and the geopolitical architecture of Europe.

NOTES

1.   The full title of the atlas is *A Concise Atlas of the Republic of Croatia and of the Republic of Bosnia and Hercegovina*, general editor, Mladen Klemencic. The atlas is produced and published by the Miroslav Krleza Lexicographical Institute, Zagreb 1993. (Authors: I. Ajanovic; L. Antic; I. Bertic; S. Bertovic; J. Bilic; D. Brozovic; M. Klemencic; V. Kusar; T. Macan; D. Majer; I. Nejasmic; E. Prelogovic; Z. Richter; J. Sentija; S. Sokol; I. Velic; J. Velic.)

2.   P. J. Taylor, *Political Geography: World-economy, nation-state and locality*, Harlow 1993.

3.   J. B. Harley, 'Deconstructing the Map', *Cartographica*, 26:2 (1989), 1–20.

4.   Benedict Anderson, *Imagined Communities*, London 1991.

5.   Klemencic, ed., op. cit., preface.

6.   ibid.

7.   Anthony D. Smith, *National Identity*, London 1991.

135

8.   'Historical Maps', in Klemencic, ed., op. cit., 94–100.

9.   ibid., 91.

10.   ibid., 79.

11.   ibid., preface.

12.   *The Europa Year Book 1993*, London 1993.

13.   See M. Thompson, *A Paper House: The ending of Yugoslavia*, London 1992.

14.   'Topographic Map', in Klemencic, ed., op. cit., 31.

15.   ibid., 88.

16.   Ivo Banac (*The National Question in Yugoslavia*, Ithaca 1984), quoted in E. J. Hobsbawn, *Nations and Nationalism since 1780: Programme, myth and reality*, Cambridge 1990, 55.

17.   D. Wood, *The Power of Maps*, London 1993.

18.   See L. Aikman, 'New Stars for Old Glory', *National Geographic Magazine*, 66:1 (1959), 86–121.

19.   Klemencic, ed., op. cit., 3.

20.   *Europa Yearbook*, op. cit.

21.   Misha Glenny, 'War Returns to Europe', *New Statesman and Society*, 9th August 1991, 11.

22.   J. B. Harley, 'Cartography, Ethics and Social Theory', *Cartographica*, 27:2 (1990), 1.

16

Maxine Hong Kingston:
'the one with the tongue cut loose'

Dominic Williams

It seems appropriate, in trying to situate Maxine Hong Kingston, to note that this California-born, first-generation American daughter of Chinese immigrants lived for a number of years in Hawai'i. In making such a move, she effectively moved eastward westwardly, remaining in the United States while being as close as possible to China. She has since returned to live in Berkeley, and it is from this location that she is currently working on what she calls her 'peace book'. Her first novel, *Tripmaster Monkey – His Fake Book*, was published in 1989. Its title pointedly echoes a charge levelled against her by Frank Chin who, in the early 1970s, had been among the editors of *Aiiieeeee! An Anthology of Asian-American Writers*. This project had been part of an attempt to restore an 'authentic' Chinese-American identity through the recuperation of an Asian-American literary tradition.[1] The attack on Kingston's 'fake book' was grounded on the fact that her characteristic mode was to distort and adapt traditional Chinese source material. She is perhaps best known for the two books in which she most dramatically deviated from the approach favoured by Chin and others. These function as companion volumes to one another: they are *The Woman Warrior*, published in 1976 (for which she won the National Book Critics' Circle Award), and *China Men*, published in 1980 (for which she won the American Book Award). It is a characteristic of both books that they interrogate tradition and explore discontinuities, dislocations, gaps and erasures, and it is from *The Woman Warrior*, a written text which explores ideas associated with acquisition of voice (and denial of such), that the idea of the tongue cut loose is derived.

Exasperated with some of her critics, Maxine Hong Kingston once said: 'the Woman Warrior is an American book. Yet many reviewers do not see the American-ness of it, nor the fact of my own American-ness.'[2] When she signs her name, she uses 'English' (or 'American') for the words 'Maxine' and 'Kingston', but retains the use of the Chinese ideogram for 'Hong', thus stressing the Chinese part of herself which is at the heart of her identity. In conversation with Timothy Pfaff, she once said: '[t]he one thing about which I am absolutely sure is that I am a Chinese-American woman. That feeling affects my writing in a particular way.'[3]

In some ways, that 'one thing' reads more like three (and, if we include 'writer', four). Certainly, the separate strands are significant each in different ways, but perhaps more significant for the ways in which they interconnect with one another to create a composite identity emerging from the fusion. In conversation with her about her first journey back to her roots (a journey on which she finally got to see the family village she had imagined so intensely), it was interesting to note the ways in which she was able to move back and forth between the two components of the 'Chinese-American identity' signalled by the words on opposite sides of the hyphen. She spoke of the occupations and invasions of 1950 and 1959 and the terrible things 'they' (meaning the Chinese) had done to Tibet. Yet, only seconds before, speaking of her visit to her ancestral village and of being welcomed back to somewhere she had never been, she had been identifying herself very strongly with the Chinese. This gives emphasis to the complexity of a 'dual identity', and, to some extent, indicates the fluidity of being both 'of' and 'other'.

I have coined the term 'fictography' to describe her work in *The Woman Warrior* and *China Men*. Both works call upon different discourses to construct a bridge between fiction and autobiography. *The Woman Warrior* is subtitled 'Memoirs of a *girl*hood among ghosts', and it is worth pausing to note that she does stress 'girlhood' rather than 'childhood'. Perhaps it is also worth pausing on the word 'memoirs'. The work, as a whole, resists easy classification and raises questions about the nature of its form. It is not a memoir in the sense of 'record of events or history written from a personal knowledge'. It is neither biography nor autobiography. Yet parts of it would seem to be biographical as in, for example, its accounts of the narrator's mother and of her dead aunt. It is 'the narrator', rather than Maxine Hong Kingston, since she herself is never named in the text, although parts of it (for example, its references to schooldays and childhood illnesses) would appear to be autobiographical. If it is a book about motherhood, it nonetheless avoids the mother's name, and she only features in the text under the name of the character 'Brave Orchid'. The aunt, whose story initiates the narrative, appears solely under the appellation 'No Name Woman'.[4] Parts of the account of the raid on No Name Woman's home echo other texts, such as contemporary newspaper accounts of the Tate/La Bianca killings. Elsewhere, the book will call upon comic books and Kung-Fu movies, privileging no particular discourse more than another as it seeks to untangle the various strands which combine to form the thread of identity.

The mother's identity is cloaked. Her aunt is only named in terms of having no name. Other than on the cover and title page, the name of Maxine Hong Kingston does not feature, leading to unavoidable speculation about how much of the narrative concerns her at all. Did she really terrorise a fellow schoolchild in the way she described, or is the incident part of the intricate design of the book, an ironic contrast to the legendary deeds of Fa Mu Lan? It is worth noting that there is a question mark over whether Fa Mu Lan is an historical person or a folk heroine. In 'White Tigers', Kingston retells very loosely a story which had been told in many forms to many different purposes. She has certainly altered the story for her own purposes, which are largely concerned with the narrator using the myth of the 'female avenger' to retell the life of a female child in an American immigrant community. In her version, the woman warrior is an ambiguous character, a woman disguised as a man in a fable of the dutiful daughter, which ends with a reconciliation to the patriarchy she seeks to subvert. Her reworking is fantasy rather than an historical reconstruction, and, it must be said, contains an element of wish fulfilment. The character Kingston calls Fa Mu Lan is usually called 'Mu Lan' and versions of the *Ballad of Mu Lan* can be traced back to the Confucian *Book of Songs* of about 600 B.C. In one translation, the story begins:

I ride, I gallop
Bearing words of comfort for the Lord of Wei,
spurring my horse on and on ...
You may oppose me
But I cannot go back.[5]

For all its use of alternative names, or its refusal to name, *The Woman Warrior* is actually a book about naming. Of the six main characters, two names (those of Fa Mu Lan and Ts'ai Yen) are rendered as transcripts of the Chinese. Two (Brave Orchid and Moon Orchid) are presented as translations of Chinese names. And, as we have seen, the remaining two have no name at all. It is a book which fixes on the idea of identity. Maybe all first books do, as the author struggles to find a voice, but, of course, one of the paradoxes of a printed text is that 'voice' will always be absent.

Yet much of the text concerns 'voice'. A good example to demonstrate the dual nature of the voice which emerges from a struggle between her Chinese and American sides might be seen in one of the stories of No Name Woman. Here, having run through various possible versions of her aunt's tale, Kingston imagines a scene in which the aunt's eyes water with pain as she plucks her eyebrows. The episode ends with a sentence which seems to move between different registers as the narrator says, 'I hope that the man my aunt loved appreciated a smooth brow, that he wasn't just a tits-and-ass man.'

The written text develops into an account of how the daughter tries to absorb her Chinese heritage through the oral discourse of her mother's 'talk story'. As a first-generation American, any attempt to recover a Chinese tradition is going to be coloured by, and, indeed, transformed by, her American experience.

Inscribed within the narrative, the mother is as much 'storytold' as 'storyteller.' She, too, has been effectively changed by her experience in America but does not always appear to be aware of ways in which this is the case. One of the stories which concerns her recounts how she effectively drove her sister over the edge into madness by trying to get her to apply Chinese village morality in the New World. It proves a dangerous and destructive mismatch, and the aunt is unable to endure the transplantation from one culture to another in which her understanding of what is correct moral behaviour seems to have no currency. As readers, it may be difficult not to ask why the mother was not more aware of the inappropriateness of her suggestions. But, for this section of the text at least, we do not have her version of events. Significantly, the source material for this tragi-comic tale does not come directly to the narrator from any of the participants. Instead, here she is seen to be relying on a story told by her brother to her sister. Several stages removed, the account she gives contains a critique of her own methodology as she goes on to point out that 'his version of the story may be better than mine because of its bareness, not twisted into designs'. Kingston once said:

> [a]ll my characters are storytellers and I suspect that some of them are telling me fictions. So, when I write their lives down, is it fiction or non-fiction? The reason that people are confused about whether my books are fiction or non-fiction is that I keep asking questions. I say, is this real? Is this true?[6]

And, as the narrative recounts her attempts to disentangle fact from fiction, it invites us, as readers, to attempt to do so too. The work allows lines to blur between different possibilities. Did this happen? Is this true? Was it really like that? Surely, this is fantasy? This is a Chinese myth, right? This isn't really a Chinese myth at all, is it? (For example, Kingston appropriates parts of the myth of the male warrior, Ngak Fei, the Patriot, for her female avenger, Fa Mu Lan, in order to allow her 'swordswoman' to become a 'wordswoman' with powerful ideograms carved into her flesh. In the transformation, she inventively generates a competing reading of the female avenger arriving 'bearing words'.) Kingston has written of her wanting to create a seamless text in which myths and lives are integrated and we cannot tell where myth leaves off and imagination and life begin. (Her approach is not without amusing difficulties. Some students of *The Woman Warrior* have expressed a wish to see its author's back in order to see what gruesome images must be carved there.)

Pushing one way with an exhortation requiring silent suffering and self-effacement, while simultaneously holding out the drum majorette as role-model, there can be few hyphenated identities more inclined to embody contradictions which seem irreconcilable than that of Chinese-American. As the text asks, at a very early point:

> Chinese-Americans, when you try to understand what things in you are Chinese, how do you separate what is peculiar to childhood, to poverty, insanities, one family, your mother who marked your growing with stories, from what is Chinese? What is Chinese tradition and what is the movies?[7]

In conversation, I asked Kingston if, on visiting China for the first time, she found that the country she was in corresponded to, or differed significantly, from the one she had invented. Her reply referred to the contradiction involved in being welcomed back to somewhere she had never been, thus signposting the wayward plurality of such oppositions as real/unreal, fiction/non-fiction, imagination/fact, indigenous/exile. Repeatedly, her prose collage invites different readings, and occasionally, the book offers different versions of the same event. In one account, her aunt is seduced. In another version, she is raped. The narrator plays with the idea of another possibility in which the aunt (whose story she has been ordered never to tell) keeps 'rollicking company'. At times, the narrator (whose telling of the story at all represents a form of betrayal) is at her most assertive at precisely those points which most depend on supposition, invention and imagination. The intensity of her imagination makes lines like the following possible:

> [o]nce my aunt found a freckle on her chin, at a spot that the almanac said predestined her for unhappiness. She dug it out with a hot needle and washed the wound with peroxide. More attention to her looks than these pullings of hairs and pickings at spots would have caused gossip among the villagers.[8]

Signposts, of course, usually point one way, but one of the features of *The Woman Warrior* is that its signs take us off in a whole series of different directions. Towards the end of the narrative, Kingston/the narrator identifies herself with the 'outlaw knotmaker', the rebellious maker of a knot which blinds with its intricacy. As 'outlaw knotmaker', Kingston twists common material into singular designs.[9] Moving between different discourses, she constructs an intricate work in which a variety of voices and perspectives interact with one another.

Much of this can be applied to the companion volume, *China Men*, where, for example, a detailed account of her father's illegal journey to New York as stowaway ends abruptly with the line: '[o]f course, my father could not have come that way', before giving way to an account of his arrival in San Francisco after an incident-free journey. While each exists in its own right, the two works are designed to complement one another. Part autobiography, part biography, part myth, part memory, part fantasy, part fiction, part non-fiction, with parts drawing on other narrative forms such as folk song, comic books and cartoons. But at least one strand of the 'knot' of both texts has nothing to do with things Chinese or things American and everything to do with gender. Her account of early family life and schooldays is, let us remember, of a 'girlhood', not a childhood. As a child, she is brought up on proverbs like 'Girls are maggots in the rice', and 'Better to raise geese than daughters'. The cautionary tale with which she begins her narrative (and which, as we have seen, she has been enjoined never to tell) is told to her as she begins to menstruate, making the transition from girlhood to womanhood. But the American girl in her frequently comes into conflict with the Chinese. Rushing home from school to announce 'I got straight As, Mama', she is greeted with the reply, 'Let me tell you a true story about a girl who saved her village.' To such a response she can only reflect: 'I could not figure out what was my village.'

To whatever sense of marginalisation she felt growing up within an American culture with quite a long history of marginalising its Chinese, must be added that sense of marginalisation Kingston felt as she spent her girlhood in a cultural background which traditionally favoured males. But how marginalised did the Chinese male immigrants feel in the New World? In *China Men*, Kingston makes reference to some casual acts of violence against Chinese immigrant workers, referring, for example, to how 21 Chinese were massacred in Los Angeles in 1872 and how, in the same year, Chinese were attached in riots in Denver. She records how 28 Chinese were attacked and murdered by a mob in Rock Springs, Wyoming, in 1885, and adds that many others were wounded and driven from their homes. It is depressing to note that much more must have gone unrecorded. It is believed, for example, that white miners in Maryville dynamited tunnels while Chinese miners were still inside. But, perhaps more frightening, because of its official inscription at Federal Government level, is her catalogue of America's anti-Chinese legislation. Here, she reminds us that the first laws to restrict immigration into the United States on the basis of race also restricted it on the basis of gender. Lucie Cheng has produced figures to show that, at the turn of the century, there were 8,217 Chinese women resident in America against a figure of 89,863 Chinese men.[10] As late as 1940, only 12 per cent of Chinese men resident in America had wives living in the country. The implications in China for this convention of absentee males involved an increasing dependence on money from abroad. Towards the end of *The Woman Warrior*, Kingston voices some doubts as the mother tears up begging letters from the youngest grandson of her father's third wife. Did her grandmother really live to be 99? Or was the American family strung along for years just to get money? What is 'cheat-story' and what is not? Who was lying? The Communists who said they had food and jobs for everybody, or the relatives who wrote that they had no money to buy salt?

Throughout *China Men*, Kingston explores a brutalisation which amounts to a kind of emasculation of Chinese male immigrants. The accounts of their lives are presented in a series of stories of suffering what is effectively a kind of institutionalised prejudice. In trying to construct her account, she cannot recover a Chinese tradition which is untransformed by the American experience. A detailed account of American laws and statutes since the Burlingame Treaty acts as a parallel commentary on the events of the narrative. Its hard facts are set in opposition to the narrative's characteristic use of camouflage, subterfuge, surprise and silences. This seems an appropriate narrative strategy, since it was exactly these kinds of ploys which enabled the immigrants to survive. But these Chinamen are also 'china men' and the narrative makes us acutely conscious of their fragility. Denied basic rights and repeatedly subjected to humiliation, they were forced to lead lives as 'married bachelors' in the New World. Bak Goong, the Great-grandfather of the Sandalwood Mountains, comments that his life is not significantly different from that of a Buddhist monk. Ah Goong achieves a rare moment of sexual epiphany as he is lowered into a ravine in a basket as part of the rock-blasting. Again, the various tales which make up the narrative interact with one another. The cumulative effect is to build up a picture of exploitation, deprivation, deception and enslavement. Yet, in telling these tales, Kingston is using her version of her ancestors' experiences to present a series of archetypes for the Chinese immigrant experience which may serve to remind her readers that these men retained enough resilience to survive undefeated and, in their various way, became warriors to match the women. Eventually, the 'brother in Vietnam' will try to demonstrate his superpatriotism by going to fight for the United States in its war in Asia. For the daughter of *The Woman Warrior*, there could be no such route to approval. Recalling how she marched and protested, the narrator sadly reflects, 'I did not turn into a boy'. Not surprisingly, the cumulative effect of such admonitions as 'Better to raise geese than girls', or 'Feeding girls is feeding cowbirds' is low self-esteem.

Contrapuntally to the scenes of the woman warrior beheading the enemy emperor comes the ironic contrast of the young girl in 'A Song for a Barbarian Reed Pipe', becoming menacing, threatening and potentially violent. Frustrated by her own inability to speak out, she externalises her fears, guilts and anxieties on to a fellow schoolmate. The irony of the distance between the glorious deeds of her fantasy life as woman warrior and the pathetic reality as she reduces her schoolmate to tears reinforces her own sense of confusion and the distance between her inner and outer selves. Bitter and angry at her own silences, her own failures to articulate, she shouts, 'Come on! Talk! Talk! Talk!' This scene may function as another strand of the blindingly complex knot of the text. Set in opposition to the intricate tying of the outlaw knot may be seen the mother's cutting of the frenum of her daughter's tongue. Scrambled up by her stories, the daughter bemoans the fact that she could not tell the difference between what was a 'true story' and what was 'just a story' and goes on to say, '[y]ou tried to cut off my tongue but it didn't work.' The mother's devastating response is to proclaim triumphantly, 'I cut it to make you talk more, not less, you dummy ... I fixed your tongue so you could say charming things.'

The alarming intervention worked. If it ever took place.

NOTES

1. See Robert G. Lee, *'The Woman Warrior* as an Intervention in Asian-American Historiography'*, in Shirley Geok-lin Lim, ed., *Approaches to Teaching Kingston's The Woman Warrior*, New York 1991, 52–63.

2. Maxine Hong Kingston, 'Cultural Mis-readings by American Reviewers', in Guy Amirthanayagam, ed., *Asian and Western Writers in Dialogue: New cultural identities*, London 1982, 55–65.

3. Timothy Pfaff, 'Talk with Mrs. Kingston', *New York Times Book Review*, June 15th 1980, 25–7.

4. My choice of Hawthorne's word 'appellation' is quite deliberate, since much of No Name Woman's story has very strong echoes of Hester Prynne, who also refused to name her inseminator and took her secret to the grave.

5. Kathryn Van Spanckeren, 'The Asian Literary Background of *The Woman Warrior*', in Lim, ed., op. cit., 45. See also Confucius, trans. Yang Xianyi, Gladys Yang and Hu Shiguang, *The Book of Songs*, Beijing 1983.

6. Phyllis Hoge Thompson, 'This is the Story I Heard: A conversation with Maxine Hong Kingston', *Biography*, 6:1 (1983), 4.

7.   Maxine Hong Kingston, 'No Name Woman', *The Woman Warrior*, London 1981, 13.

8.   ibid., 16–17.

9.   Clive Meachen, of the Department of American Studies, University of Aberystwyth, delivered an excellent paper on this theme at the Liverpool Institute of Higher Education's *Race Conference Week*, October 1989, which, to the best of my knowledge, remains unpublished.

10.   Lucie Cheng and Edna Bonacich, eds., *Labor Immigration under Capitalism: Asian immigrant workers in the United States before World War II*, Berkeley 1984. See also Robert G. Lee, 'The Origins of Chinese Immigration to the United States, 1848–1882', in *The Life, Influence and Role of the Chinese in the United States, 1776–1960*, San Francisco 1976, 183–93.

17

Writing and English national identity

Antony Easthope

'The idea of the nation is the most materialist of ideas.'[1]

The great English adventure (bourgeois, imperialist, post-Renaissance), which began so stunningly in the seventeenth century, is now coming to an end. Naturally, that crisis is signalled in the status of the monarchy. Here is the notorious Richard Littlejohn, writing in *The Sun*, on 9th November 1992:

> **Put a Sock in it, Diana**
>
> In the overall scheme of things it makes little difference whether Di is sharing a bed with Prince Charles or the Harlem Globetrotters. Mind you, she might not look so miserable if she was snuggling up to the Harlem Globe-trotters for an evening ... Why do they persist with this farcical marriage? Say what you like about Fergie, but she did have the bottle to get out. I have always preferred Sarah to Diana. She never made any bones about being a gold-digging bimbo ... Diana has come to believe her own publicity. She really does think she is a cross between Jerry Hall and Mother Teresa. Give me Jerry Hall any day. At least she has a bit of conversation. And I can live without miracles. It was always an unlikely match. Imagine you are a 19-year-old Sloane Ranger with a half-decent boat race and a figure out of a Slim-Fast commercial. You have the option of going out with a few randy racing drivers of your own age or an old man who looks like Biffo the Bear and talks to trees. Who would you choose? Be honest. Diana made a career decision. She made her own bed and now she doesn't want to lie in it.

In the genre of popular journalism, this is a text full of jokes and matey colloquialisms, with a touch of Cockney ('boat race' for face). It is based on a rhetorical opposition between the apparent and the real, so that when Littlejohn says that 'in the overall scheme of things it makes little difference' he really means it makes no difference; 'she might not look so miserable' in bed with several large African-Americans means she would be a lot happier.

What seems and what is extends into a moral schema: Diana's calculating hypocrisy is self-deceiving when contrasted to Sarah's frank self-interest, dogma (Mother Teresa's 'miracles') is rejected in favour of common sense (Jerry Hall). Littlejohn assumes that under a genteel surface we all act out of the same real and knowable motives ('Diana made a career decision'). He appears to say it right out, with blunt honesty, but we know from his exuberance he is really being irreverently polemic.

The main obstacle to analysing national culture, especially in an English context (and this is symptomatic), is a belief that nation is somehow not material, not real. In the first place there is a left-liberal prejudice, with strong antecedents in Marxism, that nationalism is (to put it crudely) a hegemonic deception organised by the ruling class in order to mask its own power. National identity is not real because it is really just an exercise in class domination.

Tom Nairn has opposed this one-sided and reductive view of nation. Contrasting 'black' and 'white' nationalism – on the one hand, Nazism soaked in the worst excesses of barbarism, on the other, the Vietnamese struggle for independence – he argued that national identity was not just imposed, but spontaneously lived into and supported, for example in the fight for national liberation.[2] Anthony Smith writes:

> [o]f all the collective identities in which human beings share today, national identity is perhaps the most fundamental and inclusive. Not only has national*ism*, the ideological movement, penetrated every corner of the globe; the world is divided, first and foremost, into 'nation-states' – states claiming to be nations – and national identity everywhere underpins the recurrent drive for popular sovereignty and democracy, as well as the exclusive tyranny that it sometimes breeds. Other types of collective identity – class, gender, race, religion – may overlap or combine with national identity but they rarely succeed in undermining its hold, though they may influence its direction.[3]

On 2nd May 1994, when Nelson Mandela first spoke as elected President of a democratic South Africa, addressing himself to '[m]y fellow South Africans', he affirmed: '[w]e might have our differences, but we are one people with a common destiny in our rich variety of culture, race and tradition.' Nation is the mode of collective identity emerging with modernity, and for the foreseeable future.

A second version of the unreality of nation claims they are imagined communities. Eric Hobsbawm refers to 'the unavailability of *real* human communities', and asks why, having lost these, people should 'wish to imagine' nations as their replacement.[4] This typically nostalgic belief is that the pre-national community was somehow face-to-face, primary, originary, and real, while national communities are second-hand, derivative, imagined, and fake. We post-structuralists have to surrender this very desirable binary, for we know that lack is universally constitutive, a signifier always represents the subject for another signifier, and there is no 'real' human community living in some Utopian world outside the sign.[5]

A third difficulty in the path of analysing nation follows from the prejudice, widespread among sociologist and historians, that economic, social and political forces are real but discourse, culture and identity is spiritual, subjective, and outside serious discussion. That is the left deviation, and it corresponds to the rightist view that national culture is only moral, spiritual and subjective. I understand Englishness as a material rather than ideal formation. National cultures are material in that they are produced through institutions, practices and traditions which historians and sociologists can describe. But national cultures are also reproduced through narratives and discourses about which those social sciences feel inhibited, but which recent theory makes a matter of coherent analysis. As the crisis of Englishness grows, the shelf of books grows with it.[6] I will begin with the issue every discussion of nation assumes but hardly ever attempt to analyse: the question of collective identity.

All human identity is collective, individual and social. To use the discourse of Jacques Lacan, the singular subject finds identity by misrecognising itself as an ego, a unified and individual self; the group subject identifies with others when individual egos become aligned and equated in common identification with a privileged figure or idea. In *Group Psychology and the Analysis of the Ego,* Freud asserts that members of the Christian Church share a common identification with Jesus, and in an army soldiers identify with their military leader. Since group identity is so much an effect of identification it diminishes sexual feeling, though Freud elsewhere points to sublimated homosexual desire as constitutive of that great patriarchal grouping, the male bond.

Human groups are constituted in a process which defines an outside against an inside. Just as the individual ego is brought about through the mechanisms of disavowal and denial until the 'I' is defined over against the 'Other', so the group identifies itself as an 'us' over against a 'them'. As Freud points out, the process exaggerates differences in the Other, 'the Englishman casts every kind of aspersion upon the Scot',[7] while differences within the group are elided or overlooked in the name of an imaginary unity. John Stuart Mill writes, '[a] portion of mankind may be said to constitute a Nationality if they are united among themselves by common sympathies which do not exist between them and any other.'[8] As I would prefer to phrase this, it is the 'Other' which lends, bestows, provides the grounds for identity, an identification which has as its main effect that we think the 'Other' is different because we know who we are.

E pluribus unum: Englishness is an effect of unity won from the effacement of actual differences – no one is purely English, not even the Queen. If one wanted to play the racial/ethnic game, one would have to admit that the English have bloodlines mingling Celts, Romans, Germanic Angles and Saxons, Nordic Jutes, Vikings and Norman French, and that only takes you to 1500. Inscribed within a specific discursive formation, Englishness is a point of identification desired precisely because it is structured by absence or lack. English identity is queer identity – but so is all identity.

Every subject has always been defined in and through a number of identities, laminated together simultaneously. Outside the family, identities extend in concentric circles into work and leisure, ethnic and sub-cultural as well as local and regional identities and, above the national register, continental and potentially international identities. National identity is only the most recent and most devastatingly intense of group identities, dependent for its introduction on the historical novelty of the nation-state. That field is well turned over, especially by historians, and especially by those writing since 1945.

The story runs like this. Before nations there were clans, tribes, lineage groupings, all kinds of ethnic and regional communities. Analysts point to the following cluster of shared features in pre-national groupings: customs; ethnic similarity; language; political organisation; religion; territory. In the West, increasingly with the Renaissance under the umbrella of Absolutism, the nation-state began to develop on the basis of a syndrome of institutions: a single market, standing armies, a bureaucracy, a system of national taxation, a consistent system of law. After 1776 and 1789 industrialism, urbanisation and *laissez-faire* capitalism – in a word, modernity – intensified the process, and the modern nation-state defined itself according to three principles: 1) political sovereignty rests with the people, not a monarch; 2) the new state is independent and self-governing; and 3) the political entity of the state is to be identified with the national culture – 'nation' *is* 'the people'. Overall, as Eric Hobsbawm says, the individual came to be 'no longer definable as the locus of a complex of multiple loyalties, but overwhelmingly in terms of a single one, his [sic] nationality.'[9]

With a surprising degree of consensus, historians agree that what is unique about national identity is its absolute and categorical nature. E. H. Carr can stand for many here when, with the American and French Revolutions in mind, he writes:

[t]he 'democratisation' of nationalism imparted to it a new and disturbing emotional fervour. With the disappearance of the absolute monarch the personification of the nation became a necessary convenience in international relations and international law. But it was far more than a convenient abstraction. The idea of the personality and character of the nation acquired a profound psychological significance.[10]

Most theories of modernity point to a narrative which goes like this: once upon a time there was an organic community rooted in the origins of human history, a community based in unchosen relations in which (apparently) everyone knew everyone else and was bound into a series of collective rituals and obligations. Along came modernity and changed all this into a society mechanically organised on rational principles, in which the world is full of strangers to whom you owe nothing unless you decide to bond with one of them. As a species we need to survive and reproduce but we are bound by an equal necessity as speaking subjects to be recognised by the Other. The crisis of modernity can be phrased in terms of identity and identification. Here I am in my eighteenth-century English village where a small, relatively closed community reflects back to me a strong and relatively stable sense of who I am, one to which I can imagine few alternatives; now I am walking down a street in Manchester in 1844 where, as Frederick Engels puts it so eloquently, I am a 'monad', bound to others only by the rule of not bumping into them, though free to wander where I want, my horizons unlimited. National identity promises to present the state as culture, an atomised society as a living human community, the socially constructed as direct experience. And so, amid the proliferating estrangements of modernity, nation would reflect back to me an effect of identity as a total presence.

I would therefore read national identity alongside the other unprecedented forms of identity which came on offer with modernity: a newly portable 'internalised' identity as free standing and freely expressive Romantic self; identity as mirrored in the recently-invented domain of Art; identity as the Romantic lover imaged in the dyadic misrecognition that there is a sexual relation. Along with these, I suggest, comes desire for an all-encompassing national identity, and so, to *be* English.

Where, then, to begin in thinking about Englishness? Where to end? Since it constitutes a feature of everything not specifically assigned to another national culture, Englishness tends to lose specificity. Looking at subjectivity and discourse, I will argue that the English national subject is a position held in place by, on the one hand, a version of the national narrative, and on the other, by a discursive formation which promotes certain discursive effects by denigrating others. These are the pins which – temporarily – nail the upholstery to the frame of this old settee.

As the crisis for Englishness worsens, efforts to define it become ever more strenuous. In April 1993, in a speech on Europe, the British Prime Minister, John Major, presented a vision of the essence of Englishness, speaking of 'long shadows on the county [cricket] grounds, warm beer, invincible green suburbs, dog lovers ... an old maid bicycling to Holy Communion through the morning mist'. Another take, from the novelist, Margaret Drabble, is: 'England's not a bad country – it's just a mean, cold, ugly, divided, tired, clapped out, post-imperial, post-industrial slag-heap covered in polystyrene hamburger cartons.'[11]

Both Major and Drabble give us lists, and a list is not a narrative – it comprises some of the possible elements from which a consequential narrative may be constructed. In one account of narrative, these static (or paradigmatic) features consist of *indices* and *informants* strung together in the (syntagmatic) narrative by *catalysers* and *cardinal functions*.[12] While there is an almost infinite number of different ways you could mix and match your own impressionist picture of England from paradigmatic features, the national narrative is, I think, much more susceptible to definable analysis. And much more important to the national culture.

In a famous lecture of 1882, Ernest Renan dismissed most of the conventional assumptions about the basis for national culture – genetic similarity, language, religion, community of material interest, geography, proposing instead that 'a nation is a soul, a spiritual principle'.[13] Renan explains this spiritual principle by saying:

> [t]o have common glories in the past and to have a common will in the present; to have performed great deeds together, to wish to perform still more – these are the essential conditions for being a people ... A nation is therefore a large-scale solidarity, constituted by the feeling of the sacrifices that one has made in the past and of those that one is prepared to make in the future.[14]

In autobiography, the narrative of individual identity, I construe my memories to imagine who I will be and so gain a sense of who I am. Similarly, the national narrative recalls past events for us so we may imagine a future which confers an identity on us in the present. I participate in a national culture to the extent that I identify myself as a subject of the national narrative.

It is obvious, however, that the national narrative is endlessly contested, that there are (to borrow a familiar taxonomy) dominant, subordinate and emergent versions of the national narrative. John Major's pastoral story of England partakes of the dominant narrative which Drabble's urban history opposes. What do the different narratives share, and what events and attitudes might they have in common? Does 'the' national narrative exist only in conflicting versions of itself? As a story, the national narrative must have a beginning and a middle, though it will have no end. Accordingly, it can be discussed in terms of its point of origin and the cardinal functions across which it is linked together. What goes into and what is excluded from the sequencing of the national narrative? The principle, as one would expect, is that Dunkirk goes in but Drogheda and Dresden stay out. Do the exclusions constitute an authentically oppositional alternative to the national narrative or is it rather that there is something like a consensus on SAVE versus DELETE and, as with 1966, it is the reading of the agreed events which counts?

There must be several tens of thousands of histories of England – from children's school histories such as Arthur Mee's *Our Island Story*, to golden oldies such as Clarendon, Macaulay and J. R. Green, as well as some of the drier and more hard-edged narratives, such as Maitland and Pollock's *The History of English Law* (1895). What matters is how the corpus is interrogated. As the concept of metahistory insists, a historical narrative is characterised by modes of emplotment, argument and ideological implication. A topic for investigation, then, would be the *nature* of the cardinal functions in the historical narrative, the *kind* of causality presumed in the sequencing of the events that are included. Is the English narrative national in the sense that, no matter whether it is written from left, right or centre, the notion of causality relied upon is empiricist? That is, that it rests upon a sense of agreement or consensus felt to lie beyond rational investigation?

Most thinking about Englishness (and national cultures) is interested in symbols, like the Union Jack, or practices, like cricket and dancing round the Maypole. But that approach stays very much at the level of content. Englishness is produced and reproduced through a discursive formation. In the 1960s, the New Left was led by Perry Anderson and Tom Nairn to criticise the English tradition for its empiricism:

[t]he hegemony of the dominant bloc in England is not articulated in any systematic major ideology but is rather diffused in a miasma of common-place prejudices and taboos. The two great chemical elements of this blanketing English fog are 'traditionalism' and 'empiricism': in it, visibility – of any social or historical reality – is always zero.[15]

Not to be confused with 'the factual' or 'the empirical', empiricism is the epistemological belief that the real can be experienced and understood more or less directly by the unprejudiced observer. Empiricism functions in a scenario with three terms, these governing the object, the means of representation, and the subject. First, the object is assumed as existing in a real which is supposedly pregiven. All you have to do is observe the real 'objectively', that is, without prejudgment or self-deception, and the real will yield knowledge of itself. As is well known, Boswell and Johnson, after coming out of church, stood talking about Bishop Berkeley's idealism until Johnson, 'striking his foot with mighty force against a large stone', exclaimed, 'I refute it *thus*'.[16] Johnson's boot has the full weight of Englishness behind it. Second, the means of representation by which the object is represented to the subject is presumed not to interfere – or to intervene only minimally – with the subject's access to the real. In principle, discourse is transparent so that the only problem for knowledge is, as it were, to go and look and see what things are *there*. Third, as always in an epistemological scenario, subject and object are joined reciprocally, so that the English subject and the English real correspond to each other. In that the English real is simply autonomous, given, the English subject is similarly not constructed but always already merely *there* as the subject of or for knowledge and/or experience.

Another immediate line of inquiry is encouraged by this. Isn't the English subject pre-eminently envisaged as a *moral* subject? Empiricist discourse would promote this according to the following logic: to see and know the real as it is (objectively) constitutes the basis for right action; to allow desire and fantasy to interfere with your treatment of the real is to view it subjectively and so be guilty of self-deception.

An example of this might be taken from Milton's *Paradise Lost*, surely a foundational text for Englishness. According to the ancient poets, Mulciber was thrown out of heaven by Jove, and at one point the poem lingeringly describes how: 'from Morn/To Noon he fell, from Noon to dewy Even/A Summer's day' (Book I, 742–4), until this soft pagan story is cut off round the end of the line in a single brutal word: 'thus they [the pagan poets] relate/Erring'. The text evokes and enjoys Mulciber's floating skydive only to reject that delight as surely as Mulciber was thrown out of heaven. Pleasure is found in the denial of pleasure, the desire is to eradicate desire. In the Milton passage we see desire becoming separated from itself by an opposition which privileges truth over error, a realistic grasp of the facts over any self-deceiving wish for fantasy. I surmise that English empiricist discourse maintains itself on the back of a metaphysical opposition between the real and the apparent reproduced and reworked in many directions: objective/subjective; concrete/abstract; in practice/in theory; clear/obscure; serious/silly; common sense/dogma; sincere/artificial; and amateur/professional. Truth – so often 'hard' truth – is opposed to pleasure. Thus, in what seems to me a peculiarly English inflection, the cognitive and the ethical overlap, a matter of truth or falsehood is always a matter of *right* and *wrong*. None of these oppositions is held in place merely by a formal logic – each relies on a field of forces for its upkeep.

I think it can be shown that certain key oppositions – common sense/dogma, serious/silly – bear with them connotations derived from Protestant/Catholic, and so in one strand of association, English/French, and so home/foreign. All of the oppositions have a tendency to map onto and equate with masculine/feminine. In this series Englishness characterises masculinity as realistic, objective, clear, serious, sincere, and right because it cleaves unrelentingly to fact while femininity is relegated as subjective, obscure, silly, dogmatic, artificial, because it is prone to fantasy, self-deception and being wrong. As Virginia Woolf said, 'As a woman, I have no country'.[17]

English empiricist discourse, following the philosophic precedents monumentalised by Bacon, Hobbes and Locke, seeks to refer to the real without rhetoric. There are three main variations of this: the straightforward 'plain style', classic irony (which refers to the real indirectly), and English Romantic poetry, in which a subject has direct experience of the real. I speculate that one of discourses standing at the margins of English empiricist discourse is what I think of as English silly discourse (*A Midsummer Night's Dream*, Lewis Carroll, *The Wind in the Willows*, Tolkien). But even that depends on empiricism for its pleasurable transgressiveness – fantasy known to be fantasy and not a reflection of the real.

My example of empiricist discourse is in the form of classic irony. Here is Andrew Rawnsley's 'Sketch' from *The Guardian* on the State Opening of Parliament, set against the earlier passage from Richard Littlejohn in *The Sun*:

Nobs in finery usher in classless society

The Lord Chancellor was trying to walk backwards without tripping over the Rouge Dragon Pursuivant, animated playing cards were blowing trumpets, Black Rod was getting the door slammed in his face like a Jehovah's Witness, and Her Majesty was straining to convince the nation that she really was looking forward to a visit from the president of Portugal.

By the grace of God and the electoral system, the Queen presided over the State Opening of Parliament, the seemingly centuries-old ceremony which traditionally ushers in another five years of Conservative government. As Beaumont Herald Extraordinary, Gold Stick in Waiting, The Keeper of the Gilded Bidet and the rest of the cast of *Iolanthe* did their stuff before an audience of dukes, earls, marquesses and viscounts, Her Majesty outlined her government's plans to create a modern, open and classless society.

It did not cause the slightest tremor of apprehension among the glorification of hierarchy assembled in the House of Lords. They thought they already understood what John Major meant when he talked about letting wealth cascade down the generations. Most of it was cascading down the diamond encrusted cleavages of peeresses.

The apparent and the real here includes a contrast between masquerade and the body: the Lord Chancellor tries not to trip over his dress, Black Rod has the door slammed in his face, Her Majesty was 'straining' her voice to sound sincere. False appearance is also marked by equating the apparent with textuality known to be textuality: 'animated playing cards' refers the scene to *Alice in Wonderland*, '*Iolanthe*' matches it to comic opera. A reference to a Jehovah's Witness rests on the same opposition between dogma and common sense as Littlejohn's jibe at 'miracles' and 'Mother Teresa'. The Queen's power is apparently named via the zeugma between 'the grace of God' and 'the electoral system', but this classic irony points the reader from what it says, to the knowledge that sovereignty rests with Parliament rather than the monarchy. Ironic also is the straight-faced allusion to ancient ceremony ushering in more Conservative government (it doesn't) and how the Keeper of the Gilded Bidet will create a modern, classless society (he won't).

Irony, but irony to what purpose? In empiricist fashion the text refers to a real by showing discrepancy between the apparent and the real – almost the apparel and the real. If the 'Sketch' had a consistent social commitment the irony would add up, resulting in satire. But this irony remains merely personal, goes nowhere except to demonstrate the writer's superior awareness of what's 'really' going on.

Littlejohn and Rawnsley illustrate comic irony in two different class registers. Rawnsley eschews Littlejohn's plain speech in favour of urbanity, educated references, elaborated vocabulary, complex sentence structure. Both texts, however, deploy the real/apparent opposition and appeal to an empiricist real. Whereas Littlejohn's claim to honesty denies his own rhetoric, Rawnsley does not try to conceal his rhetoric, as when he likens the idea of wealth cascading down to diamonds cascading down cleavages. Such rhetorical display is recuperated as personal expression. This is classic English whiggery.

Engagement with the contemporary is demanded because in part my aim is polemic, addressing the present with some intention of altering it. How does contemporary discourse relate to its inheritance? The great English foundational moment, textual innovations of the period 1650–1700, are still alive and kicking in contemporary forms, Pope's ironies at work in higher journalism, Dryden's comedy in David Lodge, Miltonic pathos in Orwell. Englishness, like ideology, works behind your back, writing you when you think you are speaking in your own voice. Thus, in the *fin de* millennium, Englishness as a topic attracts speculative reason – it is there but unexamined or insufficiently examined. But Englishness is also a political issue since a Janus-faced national culture looks back to Empire and fails to confront a European identity. I wish to argue that the present English struggle for modernisation, epitomised in Charter 88's campaign for constitutional rights, is in one respect a struggle to walk out of Perry Anderson's fog of English empiricism into the clear daylight of rationalism, from a constitutionality rooted in precedent to one codified in explicit legislation. Here is a rallying cry for England: 'Forward to 1776 and 1789'.

There is a third reason for studying national culture. It poses the most urgent but unanswered question of our time: to be human means you have to have a group identity but how can we be inside our group except by denigrating outsiders? How can we be ourselves without aggression towards the 'Other' on whom our identity depends? This is a question signalled by the work of Levinas and Derrida, and renders critical analysis of Englishness part of a larger debate over identities inscribed by class, race, gender, sexuality. Showing that Englishness is an effect is to show that it can be faked, replicated, impersonated. For if Englishness is an effect it can be changed.

NOTES

1. Regis Debray, 'Marxism and the National Question', *New Left Review*, 105 (September/October 1977), 29.

2. Tom Nairn, *The Break-up of Britain: Crisis and neo-nationalism*, London 1977.

3. Anthony D. Smith, *National Identity*, London 1991, 143.

4. Eric Hobsbawm, *Nations and Nationalism since 1780: Programme, myth, reality*, Cambridge 1990, 46.

5. See the critique of Lévi-Strauss in Jacques Derrida, *Of Grammatology*, Baltimore 1976, 101–40.

6. See, for example, Perry Anderson, *English Questions*, London 1992; Geoffrey Elton, *The English*, Oxford 1992; Roy Porter, ed., *Myths of the English*, London 1992; Eric Hobsbawm and Terence Ranger, eds., *The Invention of Tradition*, Cambridge 1983; Patrick Wright, *On Living in an Old Country*, London 1985; Robert Colls and Philip Dodd, eds., *Englishness: Politics and Culture 1880-1920*, London 1986; W. D. Rubinstein, *Capitalist Culture and the Decline in Britain 1750-1990*, London 1993; Martin Wiener, *English Culture and the Decline of the Industrial Spirit, 1850-1980*, Cambridge 1981. Among more obviously 'oppositional' studies are: Centre for Contemporary Cultural Studies, eds., *The Empire Strikes Back*, London 1982, and Paul Gilroy, *There Ain't No Black in the Union Jack*, London 1987.

7. Sigmund Freud, *Group Psychology and Analysis of the Ego*, Harmondsworth 1985, 131.

8. John Stuart Mill, *Representative Government*, London 1954, 359.

9. Eric Hobsbawm, cited in Peter Worsley, *The Three Worlds: Culture and world development*, London 1984, 255.

10. E. H. Carr, *Nationalism and After*, London 1945, 8–9.

11. Margaret Drabble, *A Natural Curiosity*, Harmondsworth 1989, 308.

12. See Roland Barthes, 'Introduction to the Structural Analysis of Narratives', in *Image-Music-Text*, London 1977, 79–124.

13. Ernest Renan, 'What is a Nation?', in Homi Bhabha, ed., *Nation and Narration*, London 1990, 19.

14. ibid.

15. Perry Anderson, 'Origins of the Present Crisis', *New Left Review*, 23 (January/February 1964), 26–53.

16. James Boswell, *Life of Dr Johnson*, New York 1945, 130.

17. Virginia Woolf, *Three Guineas*, London 1992, 313.

Notes on contributors

Simon Barker teaches English at Cheltenham and Gloucester College of Higher Education. His main research and publishing is in the area of early-modern militarism and cultural theory. He has just completed a new edition of John Ford's *'Tis Pity She's a Whore* for Routledge, and is working on a collection of essays on Shakespeare's problem plays for Macmillan.

Tracy Brain is a lecturer in English at Bath College of Higher Education. She has written essays on contemporary women's writing, including the work of Rose Tremain, A. S. Byatt, Paula Meehan and Margaret Atwood. She is currently writing a book on new approaches to Sylvia Plath's work.

Antony Easthope is Professor of English and Cultural Studies at Manchester Metropolitan University. His writing includes *Poetry as Discourse* (Methuen, London 1983), *What a Man's Gotta Do* (Paladin, London 1988), *British Post-structuralism* (Routledge, London 1988), and *Literary into Cultural Studies* (Routledge, London 1991).

Colin Edwards is Senior Lecturer in English and Creative Studies in English at Bath College of Higher Education. He has published articles on Ford Madox Ford, Ezra Pound and Wyndham Lewis, and is currently writing a book on Ford Madox Ford.

David Ellis is a lecturer in English at the University of Derby. He received his first degree at the Hatfield Polytechnic and completed a doctoral thesis on Black British literature at Essex University. His current research interests are in New Literatures in English, post-colonial theory and contemporary popular culture.

Clare Hanson is Reader in English at the University of Leicester. She is the author of *Katherine Mansfield* (with Andrew Gurr), *Short Stories and Short Fictions, 1880–1980* and *Virginia Woolf* (Macmillan Women Writers). She has also edited *The Critical Writings of Katherine Mansfield* and a collection of essays, *Re-reading the Short Story*. She has written numerous articles on women's writing and on feminist literary theory, and is currently writing a book on women and fiction after Woolf.

Tom Herron is a lecturer in the Department of English at the University of Aberdeen. He is currently writing a doctoral thesis on *The Field Day Anthology of Irish Writing*.

Tracey Hill is a lecturer in English at Bath College of Higher Education. She is co-editor (with Alan Marshall) of *Fins des Siècles: Writing, History and Culture* (forthcoming), and has published essays on Spenser, and New Historicism and cultural history.

William Hughes is a lecturer in English at Bath College of Higher Education. He is currently working on a bibliography of Bram Stoker, and several articles on the connections between Gothic fiction and medicine. He is editor of *The Jounal of Gothic Studies*, published by the International Gothic Association.

Richard Kerridge is a lecturer in English and Creative Studies at Bath College of Higher Education. He is co-author of *Nearly Too Much: The poetry of J. H. Prynne* (Liverpool University Press, Liverpool, forthcoming 1995), and co-editor of *Writing and the Environment* (Zed Books, London, forthcoming 1996). He has published articles on 20th-century fiction and poetry, and on writing and environmentalism. In 1990 and 1991 he received the BBC Wildlife Award for Nature Writing.

Nicola King is Senior Lecturer in English at LSU College of Higher Education, Southampton. Her research is on cultural politics, psychoanalytic theory, and the representation of memory in contemporary fiction and autobiography. Forthcoming publications include essays on 'Autobiography as cultural memory' in *New Formations*, and on George Perec's *W or the Memory of Childhood* in a volume of essays on Memory in the Essex Symposia Series.

Gail Low is a lecturer in English at Staffordshire University, where she teaches post-colonial writing, Chinese cinema and popular culture. She is the author of *White Skins/Black Masks* (Routledge, London 1996, forthcoming).

Willy Maley is a lecturer in English Literature at the University of Glasgow. He is author of *A Spenser Chronology* (Macmillan, Basingstoke 1994) and editor (with Brendan Bradshaw and Andrew Hadfield) of *Representing Ireland:*

159

Literature and the origins of conflict, 1534–1660 (Cambridge University Press, Cambridge 1993). He has published several essays on Renaissance literature and on literary theory.

Tim Middleton is Senior Lecturer in Literary and Cultural Studies, and Head of the English Studies programme, at the University College of Ripon and York St. John. He is the co-editor of *Writing Englishness: An Introductory Sourcebook* (Routledge, London 1995) and is currently working on representations of masculine subjectivity in modernist and postmodernist British and Irish fiction.

Michael Parker is Senior Lecturer in English at Liverpool Hope University College. He is the author of *Seamus Heaney: The making of a poet* (Macmillan, Basingstoke 1993), and is the editor of *The Hurt World: Short Stories of the Troubles* (Blackstaff, Belfast 1995) and co-editor of *Postcolonial Literatures* (Macmillan, Basingstoke 1995). He is currently working on a book entitled *The Writers and the Troubles: Drama, fiction and poetry of the Northern Irish Troubles* (Macmillan, Basingstoke 1997, forthcoming).

Gerry Smyth is a lecturer in Cultural History at Liverpool John Moores University. He is currently working on a book on *Decolonialisation and Criticism* (from which the current chapter is taken). Other research interests include modern Irish fiction and cultural criticism, and he has published essays on James Joyce, Matthew Arnold, and Irish traditional music.

Dominic Williams is Senior Lecturer in Literary Studies at Liverpool Hope University College where his work has included participation in LIHE's Ladakh Project of educational workshops with Tibetan refugees in northern India. He is currently working towards a Ph.D in the Department of American Studies at the University of Manchester, on fictography in the works of Philip Roth and Maxine Hong Kingston.

Peter Vujakovic is Principal Lecturer in Geography in the Department of Geography at Canterbury Christ Church College. His research interests include contemporary propaganda cartography and maps in the news media, with a particular interest in media representations of Europe and nationalism. He has also undertaken research on access and mobility mapping for people with disabilities, with an emphasis on the user group as producers of maps as a form of empowerment and environmental control.

Index